AF316928

The Supernatural in Íslendingasögur
a theoretical approach
to definition and analysis

Arngrímur Vídalín
Cand. Mag. thesis
Supervisor: Rolf Stavnem
Aarhus Universitet,

2012

Tower Press
Reykjavík | Copenhagen

The Nordic Middle Ages series vol. 1

The Supernatural in Íslendingasögur

Typeset by: Arngrímur Vídalín
Tower Press, Reykjavík | Copenhagen 2012
ISBN: 978-9979-72-161-1

For my grandfather
Arngrímur Vídalín Bjarnason

Contents

Foreword

I first became interested in accounts of the supernatural at a very
early age. In fact I grew up on Icelandic folktales of encounters
with revenants, or afturgöngur, and during my first trip to Aarhus
in 2009 to attend a summer school on paganism and Christianity
organized by Pernille Hermann and Rolf Stavnem, my interest was
rekindled, not least due to Stephen A. Mitchell's lecture on the de-
monification of Óðinn in the late Middle Ages. The following summer
I returned to Aarhus Universitet to attend an intensive course titled
From Greenland to Hell, and was inspired by the many fantastic lectures given there, in particular the ones given by Jonas Wellendorf and
Daniel Sävborg on visionary literature and the so named post-classical
Íslendingasögur.

These lectures became the seeds for this thesis, which I quickly
expanded upon during my first semester as a graduate student at
Aarhus Universitet, after returning from a conference in Bergen held
by the Retrospective Methods Network, where the seedling of my
hypothesis had started to come into bloom. By the end of the semester
I had, under Rolf Stavnem's supervision, produced a preliminary
research paper on this subject, which I then pursued from another
angle during my second semester in a paper for the course *History
and Cultural Memory* taught by Agnes S. Arnórsdóttir. This thesis
paper is a thorough examination of the many rocks I turned during
these studies.

I would like to thank my supervisor Rolf Stavnem for his various
pointers and the insightful advice he provided me with. In no particular order I would also like to thank Ármann Jakobsson, Daniel
Sävborg, Agnes S. Arnórsdóttir, Gísli Sigurðsson, Marteinn Helgi

Sigurðsson, Terry Gunnell, Rudolf Simek, Torfi H. Tulinius, Christian Etheridge, Mathias Nordvig and David Carrillo Rangel, for their insight and the assistance they provided me in the writing of this paper and the various projects connected to it. Many thanks to my friends Ásgeir Berg Matthíasson, Aðalsteinn Atli Guðmundsson, Silja Rós Hauksdóttir, Halldór Marteinsson, Þórunn Þórhallsdóttir, Brynjar Smári Hermannsson, Jón Örn Loðmfjörð and Gunnar Örn Heimisson, who tirelessly listened to my extended monologues about my research. I thank my parents, Stefán Arngrímsson and Svava Kristbjörg Héðinsdóttir, for their support, my grandmother Ásta Friðriksdóttir for all her encouragement and long discussions about my topic of research, as well as my brothers Þórður Örn Arnarson and Andri Dagur Stefánsson. But first and foremost I would like to thank my partner, Eyja M. Brynjarsdóttir, for all her help, understanding and patience during the two semester long process of research it took to write this thesis.

This thesis is dedicated to my grandfather and namesake, Arngrímur Vídalín Bjarnason, an avid reader of saga literature who himself never had the opportunity for formal education and died when I was at the age of seven.

Akureyri, May 2012
Arngrímur Vídalín

1. Introduction

A good deal has been written on supernatural occurences in saga literature over the last years, not least in connection to the 13th International Saga Conference in Durham in 2006. The theme of the conference was "the fantastic in Old Norse / Icelandic literature", and it produced a considerable amount of original research on the subject. Also of note are two anthologies of research on Fornaldarsögur published in 2001 and in 2009, edited by Agneta Ney, Ármann Jakobsson and Annette Lassen.[1] They include a number of articles on the supernatural and the fantastic and have already become an invaluable source on the subject.

Most of this research, as the 2009 anthology inadvertently represents, focuses exclusively on Fornaldarsögur. Other saga genres have been left relatively untouched, especially the 'realistic' saga genres, such as Konungasögur and Íslendingasögur. Also lacking, albeit not for want of sources, are attempts at a clear definition of what supernatura in saga literature is, as opposed to what it is not, however fruitful both approaches are in themselves. In other words: where the boundary lies between normal and paranormal in the saga world in a literary sense on the one hand and – to the degree that this is possible – in the mind of the supposed audience on the other, is relatively unresearched.

To be able to define what the supernatural is, looking at the literature itself is not enough.[2] Literature is not independent of the culture

---

[1] These are "Fornaldarsagornas struktur och ideologi: handlingar från ett symposium i Uppsala 31.8 – 2.9 2001" and "Fornaldarsagaerne: myter og virkelighed: studier i de oldislandske fornaldarsögur Norðurlanda".

[2] As Stephen Mitchell put it: "It is difficult not to be drawn to these rich materials, with their vivid story lines and memorable characters, but at the same time, few

from which it springs. Iceland, like Western Europe and Scandinavia, was formally and essentially Christian in the time when the sagas were written,[3] although even this base knowledge of the prominence of Christianity is not as unproblematic as it sounds.[4] It is generally assumed that "the complex set of late medieval Nordic beliefs [...] evolved from (and within) native traditions under heavy influence from imported views brought by Christianity," yet information on pre-Christian beliefs is problematic to interpret.[5] Therefore, for the purposes of this paper, I will mostly look to the formally accepted belief system of Christianity as a comparative cultural balance point, as Iceland was neither culturally nor religiously independent from the Church. I will first look to contemporary Christian world view and theology and analyse the supernatural as a whole in light of it. Once such a comparison has been made, I will use it as a basis for a deeper analysis of the supernatural within the literature.

My mode of analysis is a presupposed narrative function of three defined genera of beings found in the Íslendingasögur, which for the sake of simplicity are respectively grouped by their most signifying term: draugar (ghosts), tröll (trolls) and ófreskjur (monsters).[6] The

scholars today accept at face value that these mainly thirteenth-century texts mirror with accuracy the actual belief systems of the farmers, traders, raiders, concubines, and kings of the Viking Age. Many layers of selection, interpretation, and obfuscation lie between us and that world, just as they did for the medieval Icelanders." Mitchell, Stephen A. 2011, p. 27.

[3]The oldest extant saga manuscripts were written in the 13th century, more than 200 years after the formal christianization of Iceland around the millennium 999-1000.

[4]Mitchell, Stephen A. 2011, p. 26.

[5]Mitchell, Stephen A. 2011, pp. 25-28

[6]Regrettably, but for the sake of brevity, witchcraft and magic have for the most part been omitted from this paper. This does not mean that I consider accounts of seiðr and fjölkynngi irrelevant to the research. On the contrary, such accounts adhere to the same narrative principle introduced here, as I will demonstrate in follow-up research on the

narrative function I presuppose can be visually represented as shown in *figure 1*.

An Íslendingasaga's narrative middle can be defined as the protagonist's place of residency, permanent or temporary. It can thus equally apply to a farm or homestead as it can be a camp or a place in which a camp is being set up. In Brennu-Njáls saga, Njáll's home is at Bergþórshváll in Landeyjar, and for the most part his narrative in the saga is based in Bergþórshváll at its center. When Njáll rides to Alþingi on the other hand, the narrative middle shifts to his encampment there. A single saga can therefore be considered to have many narrative middles: e.g. the Nordic States within Europe or Iceland within the Nordic States, the latter of which functions as the narrative frame of most Íslendingasögur, and there within we can also have a certain region within Iceland as a larger narrative middle, a farmstead within that region or the wider neighborhood etc., like concentric circles, and all these can exist at the same time, as is shown in *figure 2*. The narrative periphery, conversely, is what lies beyond the narrative middle, outside the frame of civilization that is defined by the narrative middle.

The narrative middle can in principle be considered to be a 'safe point' for the protagonist, although this in some cases turns out to not be true, not least so in the case of said Njáll who is burnt alive in his home.[7] It is the place at which the protagonist feels most safe, and by the same token, where he least suspects foul play. The main exceptions to this are narratives in which the protago-

---

supernatural on a wider scale than presented in this paper. For witchcraft, see especially: Mitchell, Stephen A. 2011, Magnús Rafnsson 2006, Matthías Viðar Sæmundsson 1996, Ólína Þorvarðardóttir 2000,

[7]Brennu-Njáls saga 1954, ch. 129.

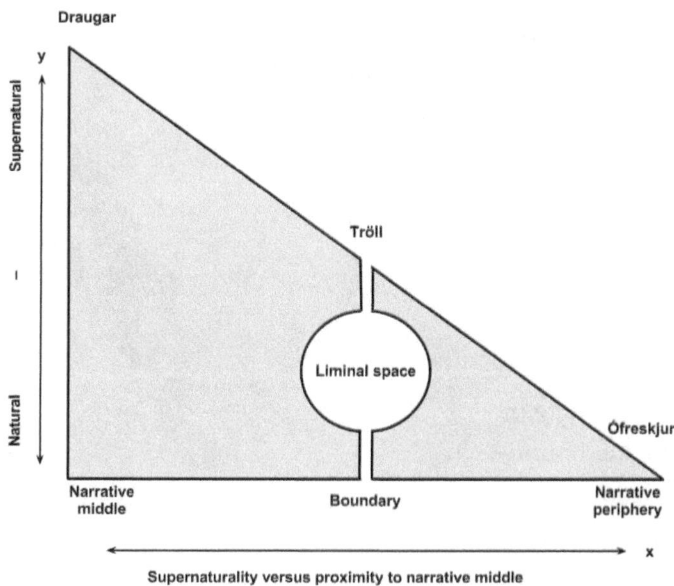

Figure 1: Narrative model

nist is outlawed and sentenced to either fjörbaugsgarðr[8] or skóg-
gangr,[9] so that he is in fact in equal danger wherever he lays his
head. Gunnarr á Hlíðarenda, to name yet another example from
Njáls saga, was sentenced to fjörbaugsgarðr and killed in his home
when he ignored the verdict.[10] Gísli Súrsson is then a countering example of an outlaw who fled his home into obscurity, and
consequently was remorselessly sought out and eventually killed.[11]

In such cases the narrative middle dissolves and becomes in a way a figurative liminal space between two points the protagonist is destined never to reach.

The liminal space as portrayed in *figure 1* lies on the boundary between the narrative middle and the narrative periphery.

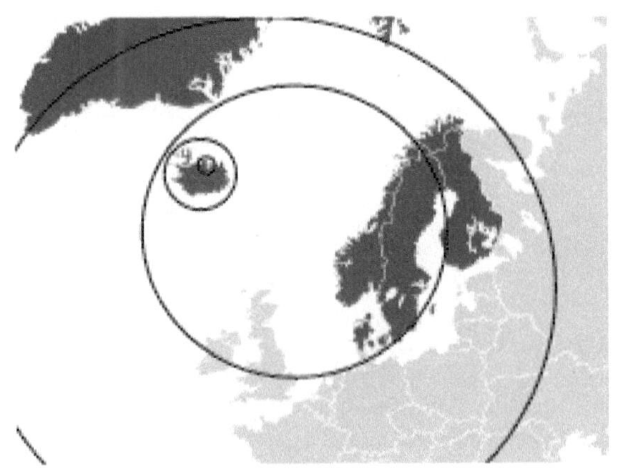

Figure 2: Concentric narrative middles

It is the geographical or spiritual place the protagonist must travel
through before either reaching a second narrative middle or the nar-

---

⁸A sentence of exile from Iceland for the duration of three years, during which time
the sentenced could be rightfully killed without consequence should he be spotted in
Iceland Grágás 1992, pp. 527-8.

⁹A sentence of life long exile from Iceland, the highest punishment during the
commonwealth era (Grágás 1992, p. 557) The sentenced could be rightfully killed on
sight wherever he was spotted for the rest of his life.

¹⁰Brennu-Njáls saga 1954, ch. 77.

¹¹Gísla saga Súrssonar 1943, ch. 26.

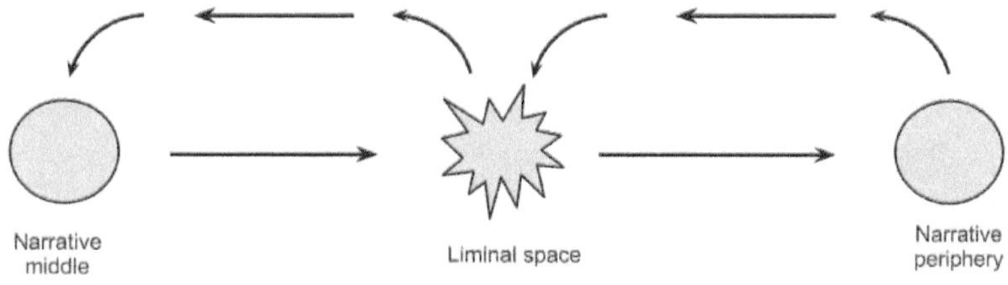

Figure 3: Structure of the travel narrative

rative periphery. On a smaller scale, this liminal space can be a cave or a mountain pass in between the protagonist's home region and e.g. Alþingi (the Icelandic parliament and tribunal). On a larger scale it can be the ocean between Iceland and Norway, and from there on it can be the forests between Norway and the uncharted areas to the east, where the narrative periphery of Íslendingasögur often lies. This structure of the travel narrative is portrayed in *figure 3*.

Along this route, from the narrative middle through the liminal space to the narrative periphery, the aforementioned beings may be found (i.e. draugar, tröll and ófreskjur) as I have attempted to show in *figure 1*. I have assumed that each genus can only be found in each respective narrative space: draugar keep to the narrative middle, tröll are to be found seasalting on both sides of the boundary or on the liminal plane, and ófreskjur like to graze on the narrative periphery. If we, then, look at *figure 1* as an xy-graph, the hypothesis states that:

1. the farther the protagonist travels from the narrative middle, the more likely it is that he will come across a) tröll, when a

liminal space is reached, and b) ófreskjur, when the periphery
is reached. Conversely, he is more likely to witness draugar the
closer he is to the narrative middle.

2. the farther the protagonist travels from the narrative middle, the
   less likely it is that he meets supernatural beings. Conversely,
   the closer he is to the narrative middle, the more likely it is that
   he will witness supernatural occurences and/or beings.

3. the assumption follows that draugar are in all ways supernatural
   and that ófreskjur are in all ways natural, while tröll rock the
   balance between the two.

This hypothesis is exclusive to the narrative function of the supernatural within the Íslendingasögur. And yet, it leads to the question of
this narrative function's basis in contemporary culture, i.e.: does it
reflect a reality outside the literature, or a world view, and if so then
to what extent? What, then, is its inherent cultural meaning?

As medieval literature, or any literature for that matter, is not
rooted outside of cultural context, the underlying assumption that:

4. this narrative function has basis in contemporary Christian world
   view

was added to the hypothesis. In an attempt to avoid superimposing
semi-fictional literature on top of the reality of medieval Europe, and
thereby deducing the culture from its literature, I will first look at
contemporary Christian world view to see if item 4 of the hypothesis
holds up to scrutiny.

2. The medieval Christian world view

2.1 Iceland within Europe: World view and classical learning

The term world view is often used in academic discourse without further explanation, but in order for its meaning to be clear, a definition is necessary. Sverrir Jakobsson has written extensively about the Icelandic world view between 1100 and 1400, e.g. in his doctoral thesis *Við og veröldin* (2005). Sverrir's definition of world view is as follows:

> Heimsmynd stendur fyrir hugmyndir tiltekins hóps, sem er afmarkaður af tungumáli, menningarlegri einsleitni eða stéttarvitund, um umheiminn í víðasta skilningi, efnisheiminn, lönd og legu þeirra og, síðast en ekki síst, þá sem þar búa. Viðhorf til annarra þjóða eru mikilvægur en vanræktur þáttur heimsmyndar. Heimsmynd hóps er samnefnari eða miðgildi margra heimsmynda einstaklinga innan hans. Heimsmynd er sjóngler sem aðrir eru skoðaðir í gegnum en endurvarpar um leið sjálfsmynd þeirra sem líta í gegnum það á aðra. Myndin af „hinum" er um leið mynd af „okkur" [...] Hinir vanræktu drættir heimsmyndarinnar eru þeir sem snúa að árekstrum menningarheima. Aðgreining á sjálfinu / okkur og hinum er grundvöllurinn sem heimsmyndir allra þjóða byggjast á.[12]

---

[12]Sverrir Jakobsson. 2005, 32-38. **My translation:** World view stands for the ideas of a particular group, which is characterized by a language, cultural homogeneity or a sense of class, of the outside world in its widest sense, the material world, countries and their location, and, last but not least, those who inhabit them. Views on other nations are an important yet a neglected part of a world view. The world view of a group is a

Kirsten Hastrup has pointed to a similar dichotomy implicit in the very notion of civilization: "The notion of civilisation implies its own negation – that which is not civilised. For civilisation to register, a negative image must be invoked, either in another time or in another space."[13] This argument fits well in with the notion of world view insofar as one entity, let us call it (a) for the sake of argument, always invokes another counter-entity (b), and vice versa; for all those who define themselves as 'normal' as opposed to an 'other', there will always be 'others' who perceive themselves to be 'normal' whereas to them the other party becomes 'the other'.

This dualism, evident in the extant written Icelandic sources, has to some extent elicited the idea that medieval Iceland was in some way secluded from the rest of Europe, culturally and politically (not to mention geographically). This view has e.g. been expressed by Sigurður Nordal:

> Axel Olrik hefur kveðið svo að orði: „Hin sérstæða menning Íslands stafar einkanlega af því, að hún er framhald fornra lifshætta, einræktuð víkingamenning. Þar gátu áhrifin af stórbrotinni reynslu víkingaaldar og samfélagshættir þess tímabils þróazt í næði. Síðari hræringar voru ekki sterkari en svo að þær ýfðu aðeins yfirborðið [. . .] Trúarlíf miðalda, kirkjuvald og konungsveldi, áhrifin af viðgangi aðalsstéttar og riddaramennta bárust ekki út til

common denominator or a median of the many world views of the individuals within that group. A world view is a looking glass through which others are inspected, yet reflects at the same time the self-portrait of those who look through it upon others. The idea of the "other" is at the same time an idea of "ourselves" [. . .] The neglected shards of the world view are those of clashing cultures. A demarcation of the self/us and the other is the foundation upon which the world views of all nations are built.

[13]Hastrup, Kirsten. 2009, 109.

Íslands nema eins og lítil ylgja." Hér er aðeins ástæða til að
nema staðar við eitt atriði í þessum ummælum Olriks: Er
réttmætt að kalla íslenzku landnámsmennina víkinga?[14]

Some may grin at this now, but it has not been so long since this was the
predominant opinion. This idea of an isolated Iceland in fact comes
from continental Europe according to Torfi Tulinius, it is the point of
view of "someone at the centre who is looking at the periphery."[15] So,
even to the small degree that the isolation of Iceland can be considered
fact (it certainly did take long to travel from Iceland to Europe), it does
inspire a number of misapprehensions about the European cultural
region in the Middle Ages. As Torfi Tulinius put it, the notion "can
be expressed by the following propositions: "the culture of medieval
Iceland is the purest conserved manifestation of Germanic culture"
and "it is not yet under the influence of Christian European culture
with its basis in Latinity"."[16] In a recent article, Rudolf Simek rejects
this same postulation that medieval Icelandic culture was radically
different from that of Europe (the notion of "two cultures") and argues
that the medieval Icelandic world view in fact was essentially Western
European. While disagreeing with Sverrir Jakobsson's "hermeneutic
and processual definition of world view", he adds that:

---

[14]Sigurður Nordal. 1993, 96. **My translation:** Axel Olrik said the following: "The
culture of Iceland is unique especially because it is the continuation of an ancient
way of life, it is a pure viking culture. There, the effect of spectacular experience of
the viking age and the social conventions of that era, could develop in peace. Later
developments were not more influential than so, that they barely rippled the surface
[. . .] Medieval religious life, ecclesiastical authority and kingship, the influence of the
nobility's success and knighthood, did not reach Iceland but in the way a tiny ripple
would on a large lake." There is only cause to voice reservations about one detail here:
Is it justifyable to call the Icelandic settlers vikings?

[15]Torfi H. Tulinius. 2009, 199.

[16]Torfi H. Tulinius. 2009, 201.

seeing that educated Medieval Christians studied much the same books all over Western Europe, it follows that much of the world view throughout Western Europe will be consistent, of course allowing for local traditions, superstitions and even mythologies that may preserve elements important to peoples' identities on a lower level than their humanity and Christianity. [17]

Simek bases his argument on a number of learned Icelandic cultural examples comparable to Europe, including the *septem artes* by which the four Icelandic grammatical treatises are indubitably inspired,[18] along with extant geometrical and mathematical writings[19] and astronomical theories derived from the Venerable Bede. Icelandic mapmaking also shows glaring connection with the European tradition and world view, while three out of fifteen surviving maps of Jerusalem are Icelandic. Simek also points out that in 'soaking up fashionable knowledge', Icelanders were far from behind Europe, as is evident in the Icelandic *Physiologus*.[20] One of its anthropomorphic species, the sciopod (or uniped), can be found in *Eiríks saga rauða*, which in Simek's view is "obviously to prove the fact that Vinland did indeed extend from Africa, a point made in the short cosmography in AM 736 I 4to (written around 1300)."[21] His strongest argument is that of a unique Icelandic table of fabulous creatures "which does not rest directly on a continental source, but presupposes a knowledge of high

---

[17]Simek, Rudolf. 2009, 184-5.

[18]See also Gunnar Harðarson. 1989, 7-19.

[19]Of extant geometrical and mathematical manuscripts, Simek names AM 194 4to, AM 685 d 4to, GKS 1812 4to and AM 764 4to as examples.

[20]The Physiologus is an allegorical (therefore Christian) work in which various beasts are given Christian meaning; these include dragons, phoenix and many more.

[21]Simek, Rudolf. 2009, 190.

Medieval teratology which then was used in a playful way elsewhere, like in the margins of *Flateyjarbók* or in copies of *Jónsbók*." [22]

On a similar note, Torfi Tulinius argues that Icelandic clerics were no less educated than their European counterparts, as they were undoubtedly all subject to classical Latin learning. According to Torfi there is overwhelming evidence to be found for European knowledge being widespread in Iceland at least from the late 11th century and onwards, and that this knowledge also was spread among the lay chieftain class.[23] Torfi demonstrates this knowledge with an example found in *Hrafns saga Sveinbjarnarsonar*:

> Hrafns saga even describes how its protagonist removes
> a kidney stone which had been obstructing the urethra
> of one of his neighbours. Scholars have shown that the
> medical acts that Hrafn is said to have accomplished are
> quite in keeping with what was being taught in the new
> schools of medicine in 12th-century Europe. [24]

Torfi then refers to Orri Vésteinsson's book, *The Christianization of Iceland*, in which one of the more interesting results is that the Icelandic Church both molded society and evolved with it, while following the same evolution as the Church did elsewhere in Europe at the same time.

Indeed, it seems impossible to speak of a secular Icelandic world view in the Middle Ages. Sverrir Tómasson argues in his dissertation that most likely the medieval Icelandic authors or scribes imitated their European colleagues. The classical rhetorics of Cicero or Quintilius are, on the other hand, never mentioned in the sources, so most

---

[22]Simek, Rudolf. 2009, 191.
[23]Torfi H. Tulinius. 2009, 202-3.
[24]Torfi H. Tulinius. 2009, 204.

likely the Icelandic scribes developed their rhetoric through the works of younger authors such as St. Augustine of Hippo, Isidore of Sevilla, the Venerable Bede or Alcuin of York.[25] What is in any case evident from *The First Grammatical Treatise*, preserved in Codex Wormianus which was "written not much later than the middle of the fourteenth century"[26] in Iceland, is that 1) it is not clearly derived from any European model, 2) that such a book could only have been written where a learned Latin culture was prominent and 3) that the author had to have learnt rhetorics either at a school in Iceland or abroad, and from that it can be deduced that he must have chosen the book's rhetoric form simply because he did not know of any better way of getting his arguments across. This would further entail that he chose this form because the treatise's intended receivers either 1) had the same or similar education as the author, which would lead to the argument that European education among the layman was common, or 2) that an argument of this kind had been common in books written in the vernacular and that European literary conventions had been more common in Iceland in the 12th century than hitherto was thought. A third option would be that the treatise was intended for fellow scholars, yet this seems to fly in the face of its intended purpose, and therefore, whichever option we chose, it would indicate that rhetorics were known in Iceland as early as the 12th century, and that it was either taught in Iceland or brought to Iceland.[27]

The formation of the first universities was already underway in Europe in the later half of the 12th century, which further adds weight to Sverrir Tómasson's argument, along with the fact that both Latin

---

[25]Sverrir Tómasson. 1988, 39.
[26]Hreinn Benediktsson. 1972, 18.
[27]Sverrir Tómasson. 1988, 39-42.

and holy scripture were already taught in Hólaskóli[28] in the first part of the same century.[29] Add to this that the oldest monastery in Iceland, founded in 1133, was of the Benedictine Order, with another one founded at Munkaþverá in Eyjafjörður in 1155; both of these were situated in the episcopal see of Hólar. In the see of Skálholt, a monastery was founded in 1166, yet not much else is known of it. In 1168, a monastery of Canons Regular, a body of priests under the Augustinian Order, was founded in Þykkvabær í Veri and another one in Flatey in 1172, which relocated to Helgafell in 1184. A cloister was then founded by nuns of the Benedictine Order in Kirkjubær in 1186, and Viðeyjarklaustur, founded in 1226 with the involvement of Snorri Sturluson and Magnús Gissurarson bishop, was of the Augustinian Order.[30]

Many books were to be found in these monasteries, including *Cura Pastoralis* by Pope Gregorius the I., along with his homilies and those of St. Augustine and Isidore, *De Doctrina Christiana* by Augustine and *Elucidarius* by Honorius Augustodunensis.[31] These are only a few mentions of many tenths or even hundreds of books which were being translated all over Europe at the same time as they were being translated in Iceland.[32] In light of this, Gunnar Harðarson comments

---

[28] The school at Hólar in Iceland, founded by Jón Ögmundsson, bishop from 1106 to 1121.

[29] Gunnar Harðarson. 1989, 10-11.

[30] Gunnar Harðarson. 1989, 14.

[31] Gunnar Harðarson. 1989, 14-15.

[32] As a side note, it is prudent to mention that some instances may give rise to scepticism, such as the case of the writer of Þorláks saga when he quotes Isidore: "at bæði er nytsamligt at nema mart ok lifa réttliga, en ef eigi má bæði senn verða þá er enn dýrligra at lifa vel." This attribution to Isidore was not verified until 2003, when it was found inconspicuously lying within his *Isidorus Hispalensis Sententiae*: "Utile est multa scire et recte vivere. Quod si utrumque non valemus, melius est ut bene vivendi

23

that:

> Eins og hér hefur komið fram eru þýðingar erlendra rita að
> heita má jafn gamlar íslensku ritmáli [. . .] Þetta býður svo
> heim þeirri spurningu hvort fremur beri að rekja hugmyn-
> dir okkar um sérstöðu Íslendinga á miðöldum til þekkingar
> á íslenskum bókmenntum eða vanþekkingar á bókmenn-
> tum annarra þjóða.[33]

The argument has sometimes been propagated, though it is mostly
extinct, that this learned culture may not have reached the ears of the
general public, as books were only accessible to the learned elite,[34]
which has spurred criticism in recent years and prompted the question
whether it is at all reasonable to assume some sort of schism between
the learned and the lay.[35] Indeed the argument is unconvincing as the
lack of ability to read or write does not preclude general knowledge
of the workings of the world. I agree with Margaret Cormack and
Aron Gurevich in that "the assumption that ecclesiastical literature
was the exclusive property of the learned class, completely cut off
from the beliefs of the majority of the population" is a spurious one
to make, as "to be successful, preaching had to take its audience into

---

studium quam multa sciendi sequamur," (Helgi Guðmundsson. 2003, 237-8) which
most certainly is a direct quote (I base this on the criteria proposed by Gísli Sigurðsson.
2002, e.g. 24, 245).

[33]Gunnar Harðarson. 1989, 18-19. **My translation:** As is shown here, the translating
of foreign books is so to say as old as the Icelandic written language [. . .] This begs the
question of whether our ideas about the uniqueness of Icelanders in the Middle Ages
should be traced to knowledge of Icelandic literature, or a lack of knowledge of the
literature of other nations.

[34]Gurevich discussed the idea as a child of the litterati-illitterati division (Gurevich,
Aron. 1988, 1-3). Cf. Mohrmann, Ch. 1955, Grundmann 1958, .

[35]Mitchell, Stephen A. 2011, 19-20.

consideraton".[36]

Gísli Sigurðsson has doubted the importance of a uniform world view of medieval Europe, but argues around the problem by pointing out that the term 'medieval' is too wide to attach any sort of uniformity to it, and that Icelanders had a different view of the world from the peoples of continental Europe as they never raised buildings of stone or had to worry about armored knights; instead they just incorporated that from ecclesiastic learning which they wanted and wrote their own stories.[37] While it is hard to argue against the latter part, the first part of Gísli's argument seems to assume for no apparent reason that the notion of a medieval world view is meant to apply to the whole of Europe from the fall of the Western Roman Empire in the 5th century to the Renaissance between the 14th and 17th centuries, rather than, e.g. as Simek applies it, to the world view of the 12th century alone.[38] Whether we like to believe in a uniform or a nonexistent world view, neither of these positions finds us sitting in the catbird seat. Just as we should be vary of the learned-lay division, we should avoid similar absolutes in discussion of world view.

The notion of world view in this context rather indicates a collection of ideas within a continental culture than a whole picture of the world common to all people. A Christian world view would thus contain similar or uniform ideas of religion, but that would not necessarily mean that tradition or individual belief would be the same everywhere. Gísli's criticism, in his firm stance against ideas of uniformity, leads him to argue against Snorri Sturluson's knowledge of Latin learning as the books generally attributed to him, *Edda*, *Heim-*

---

[36]Cormack, Margaret. 1992, 221.Gurevich, Aron. 1988, 1-8
[37]Gísli Sigurðsson. 2002, 1-3.
[38]Simek, Rudolf. 2009, 185.

skringla, and *Egils saga*[39] show little usage of this knowledge. Gísli names Faulkes' idea that Snorri could not have written like he did had he known Latin.[40] If knowledge of Latin necessarily eliminated creativity then the unique and fragile creativity of Icelanders would be a rather shaky foundation to build an argument upon, not least due to the many arguments to the contrary,[41] but first and foremost because if we accept the supposition that the creativity of Icelanders was unique, a necessary conformity of scribes or authors to Latin canons would contradict the argument.

Faulkes believes Snorri could have incorporated his world view from maps rather than Latin texts,[42] but in light of the comparatively few extant maps to manuscripts I would like to ask why that should be more probable. In contrast, Sverrir Jakobsson has argued that it is an impossibility.[43] At the very least it is not a very probable or fruitful solution to this imaginary problem, as Snorri writing about *a* does not mean he did not know *b*, and Gísli's solution that Snorri wrote independent secular literature (under obvious Christian influences I might add) does not conflict with the accepted idea that Snorri was essentially a Christian and was very well in tune with the ideas and world view of continental Christianity; on the contrary that very idea would rather support Gísli's case for Snorri's creativity. It would seem obvious to the folklorist that each region adapts religion to its indigenous culture.[44]

---

[39]That is to say if we accept Snorri's authorship of them in the first place. For a more critical approach to these attributions, see Boulhosa, Patricia Pires. 2005, 6-21.

[40]Gísli Sigurðsson. 2002, 9.

[41]Cf. Baetke 1950, Dronke, Ursula and Peter 1977, Schier, Kurt 1981, Beck 1993, Clunies Ross, Margaret 1987, Gunnar Harðarson. 1989,

[42]Cf. Gísli Sigurðsson. 2002, 8.

[43]Sverrir Jakobsson. 2005, 75-84.

[44]That is indeed to some degree the conclusion that (Bagge, Sverre. 2009) arrives at.

And such is the case of medieval Iceland. All evidence suggests that Iceland was neither isolated from the continent nor were its people from the clergy, but rather that both lay central in European culture and contemporary world view as Gísli argues for, his considerations of Snorri notwithstanding.[45] In this paper I will hence consider the world view presented in the sources, based on the arguments presented above, neither to be ethnically nor internally isolated, but that there was a medieval European world view that is tangible to the modern researcher. This is important as it gives us the possibility of correlating religious themes with literary motifs without necessarily resorting to absolutes. To do this we must assume that a certain set of properties define what Christianity is, as without assuming any kind of uniformity would undermine the very concept of Christianity as it could be made to mean anything. It follows that if Iceland in the time of writing of the sagas was Christian that their understanding of Christianity was in most respects uniform with continental understanding of Christianity, and that we should be able to trace this understanding in the literature in order to get a fuller picture of the world view it is founded upon. I will therefore use the following definition of world view:

> A culturally inherent understanding and interpretation of the physical and the spiritual world, its peoples, cultures, wildlife and nature, through geographical, theological and everyday life survey.

I shall return to this later on, but first we shall take a look at visionary and pilgrimage travel narratives.

---

[45]Gísli Sigurðsson. 2002, 22-33 Gísli has also discussed the silence on Celtic influences in Iceland to great lengths, e.g. (Gísli Sigurðsson. 2009)

2.2 Christian travel narratives: Visionary literature and pilgrimages

With a slight simplification, one can say there are two genres of religious medieval travel narratives:[46] visionary literature[47] and pilgrimage literature, the latter of which – whether the travels themselves were undertaken for the purpose of prestige, piety or to redeem oneself of one's sins – were written to convey an allegorical, religious meaning; whereas the previous contain more thinly veiled allusions to what awaits sinners at the end of their mortal lives. In this respect, both sub-genres within the genre of Christian travel narratives complement each other, with one pertaining to spiritual punishment and eventual redemption through divine intervention; the other to the quest of the pious or the morally remorseful to fulfill their religious calling and live forever by the side of their Lord in Paradise.

An example of visionary literature to be mentioned is the only originally Nordic vision[48] (though perhaps based on the *Visio Tnugdali*),[49] described in *Leizla Rannveigar*, preserved in the various redactions of *Guðmundar saga biskups*,[50] which itself is preserved in four manuscripts (A–D). It has generally been speculated that it was written before 1249, whereas Jonas Wellendorf argues that the text may have evolved to a similar form to the preserved version around the millennium 1300.

---

[46]Sverrir Tómasson counts a third kind which can either be religious or temporal: travelogues, both of saints and worldly men, of which examples may be found both in Íslendingasögur and in Dýrlingasögur (Sverrir Tómasson. 2001, 24-5.)

[47]Old Norse: *Leizla*

[48]Wellendorf, Jonas. 2009, 282.

[49]Larrington, Carolyne. 1995. It may be added that Visio Tnugdali was in fact translated into Old Norse in the 13th century (Duggals leizla), which the interested reader may find in a published edition edited by Peter Cahill with an English translation (Duggals leiðsla. Stofnun Árna Magnússonar. Reykjavík 1983).

[50]Larrington, Carolyne. 1995.

The A version is written in the first half of the 14th century, B shortly after 1320 (yet is not considered to hold up to scrutiny), C is thought to have been written between 1320 and 1345 and is based on B, yet more stylishly written than both A and B, and D is a reworking of C, with some materials added and others removed, written after 1343. The A version is the only one that has been published in a modern critical edition.[51]

The vision is supposed to have taken place in the winter of 1198 in eastern Iceland. Rannveig loses consciousness one morning after feeling immense physical pain, and when she wakes up in the evening, she asks to reveal her vision to the priest Guðmundur Arason at Víðimýri in Skagafjörður. After losing consciousness, she had been seized and tortured by demons, who burnt her legs, hands and her back, and threatened to throw her into a boiling pit surrounded by hellfire for having had affairs with two priests, and for being vain and greedy for wealth. In terror, Rannveig cried out for St. Mary and St. Peter, Ólafur helgi, Earl Magnús of Orkney and Hallvarður, patron saint of Oslo. It is interesting that only the Scandinavian saints then appear and rescue Rannveig from the demons, and then take her to see Heaven, so she may know what award awaits those who are true to their Lord and saviour. What is most interesting, however, is the explanation the saints give for the wounds – that they represent Rannveig's sinful use of the parts of her body in question (as noted by Helga Kress: "Í þessu geta bæði fjandar og helgir menn sameinast gegn konunni"):[52]

Nú brannstu því á fótum, að þú hafðir skrúðsokka og

---

[51]Wellendorf, Jonas. 2009, 290.

[52]Helga Kress 2006, 47. **My translation:** "In this, both demons and holy men can be united against the woman."

svarta skúa og skreyttist svo við körlum, en því á höndum,
að þú hefur saumað að höndum þér og öðrum á hátíðum,
en því á baki og herðum, að þú hefur borið á þig skrúð og
léreft og skreyst við körlum af metnaði og óstyrk.[53]

Moreover, her wounds are still in place when she regains consciousness, never to heal again, as a reminder of what awaits those who
stray of the path of God. Thusly, she experiences both Heaven and
Hell, and serves as a living exemplum and a warning to others; a
divine task she fulfills with admonition.

According to Margaret Cormack, the

> primary purpose of such visions (and indeed of miracles
> in which no visions occur) is to confirm the power of the
> saint and the efficacy of calling on him for aid [...] The
> other function of visions is didactic. Sinners are criticized
> for their behaviour, and may be told that they have been
> cured as a result of the piety of their loved ones rather than
> because of their own deserts.[54]

Although Rannveig probably never existed,[55] the writing of her leizla
functions equally well as an exemplum within the Christian mindset
as she herself, and her stigmata, would have done in real life. It is
not allegorical in the religious sense,[56] but a living proof of a heavenly order and a divine code of moral – no matter whether the events

---

[53]Guðmundar saga biskups 1953, 232. **My translation:** For this reason your feet were
burned, that you had fine socks on and black shoes to appeal to men; your hands, for
you sew on holy days; your back and shoulders, for you have worn fine clothes and
fabrics and made yourself appealing to men with ambition and weakness.

[54]Cormack, Margaret. 1994, 193.

[55]Larrington, Carolyne. 1995,

[56]However it most certainly is allegorical in a feministic and political sense to the
modern reader.

described are fictional or not, in very much the same way that it does
not matter whether saints in reality performed their acts of miracle,
as such thoughts never came into question, for the events and stories
documented were equally true to their audience, regardless of veracity, for otherwise they would not have been told in the first place.[57] It
must also be considered that the further removed these events were in
time from their perpetuation within oral tradition, the more legendary
credibility they must have attained in the mind of the audience (e.g.
the 120 years passing from the events of *Leizla Rannveigar* until it was
written down in its extant version). These exemplum and accounts
of miracles were in the Middle Ages, just as they still are in modern
times, an extremely important part of the Christian world view.

Pilgrimage narratives, on the other hand, are perhaps at the same
time more retrospective and historical as they are more contemporary
than the visionary literature. I would like to focus on one example, namely the documentary record of the pilgrimage undertaken
by the Benedictine monk Nikulás Bergsson of Þverá, fittingly named
Leiðarvísir.[58] It is an especially interesting piece of narrative as it
describes many mythological waypoints along the road to the eter-
nal city of Rome, allegorically imbued with theological symbolism
and meaning, as both Lars Lönnroth[59] and Peter Dinzelbacher have
observed:

> Auch der Ablauf einen menschlichen Lebens selbst wurde
> und wird schon rein sprachlich mit einer räumlichen Meta-
> pher ausgedrückt: Der Ausdruck Lebensweg oder, po-
> etischer, Lebensreise, ist in den europäischen Sprachen

---

[57]Cf. Gurevich, Aron. 1988, 1-8.
[58]Roughly translating to a road guide.
[59]Lönnroth, Lars. 1990,

gegenwärtig ganz gewöhnlich: course of life, livsvej, cammino della vita, passage/voyage de la vie usf. Das Mittelalter hat diese Metapher in Wort und Bild in narrative Szenen und Sequenzen umgesetzt – die Allegorie der Lebensreise führte durch fremde Landschaften, konfrontierte mit phantastischen Wesen und formulierte eine zentrale Komponente der mittelalterlichen Mentalität: ihre christliche Religiosität.[60]

I shall return to these "fantastic creatures" later on.

Of the many stops Nikulás mentions in his Leiðarvísir, one of the first is Gnitaheiði in Germany, where Sigurður fáfnisbani slew the dragon Fáfnir to a dramatic unfolding of subsequent events. Another one is Vífilsborg, which the sons of Ragnar loðbrók conquered after a lengthy siege and, believing themselves to be invincible, consequently set out to conquer Rome. Along their way to Rome they happen upon an old wanderer who, perhaps by an action of exercised guile, although in my view rather by circumstance or divine intervention, dissuades them from attempting to reach the city merely by showing them his boots:

Þeir spyrja hvað manna hann væri. En hann segir að hann

---

[60]Dinzelbacher, Peter. 2005, 65 **Translation:** Even the course of a human life itself was, and still is, expressed in language through a spatial metaphor. The expression Lebensweg or, more poetic, Lebensreise, is currently very common in different European languages: course of life, livsvej, cammino della vita, passage/voyage de la vie etc. In the Middle Ages, this metaphor was translated into narrative scenes and sequences in terms of words and pictures. The allegory of the voyage of life led people through foreign landscapes, confronted them with fantastical creatures, and formulated a central component of the medieval spirit: their Christian religiosity.

My best of thanks to German scholar Beeke Stegmann, who was kind enough to replace my crude translation with her own.

sé einn stafkarl og hafi alla ævi farið yfir land. „Þú munt
mart kunna tíðinda að segja oss, það er vér viljum vita."
Hinn gamli maður svarar: „Eigi vet eg það víst, af hverjum
löndum þér viljið spyrja þess er eg veit eigi að segja yður."
„Það viljum vér að þú segir oss hve löng leið er héðan til
Rómaborgar." Hann svarar: „Eg kann segja yður nokkuð
til merkja. Þér megið hér sjá þessa járnskó er eg hefi á
fótum mér, þeir eru nú fornir, og þá aðra er eg hefi á baki
mér, þeir eru nú og slitnir. En þá er eg fór þaðan batt eg
þessa á fætur mér hina slitnu er eg hefi nú á baki mér,
og voru þá nýir báðir, og á þeirri leið hefi eg verið ávallt
síðan." En er hinn gamli maður hafði þetta mælt þykjast
þeir sjá að þeir megi eigi þessu á leið koma, er þeir hafa
fyrir sér ætlað, til Róms að fara. Og nú snúa þeir frá með
her sinn og unnu margar borgir, þær er aldrei höfðu unnar
verið fyrr, og þess jarteinir sjást enn í dag.[61]

The city of Rome is thus saved from the brothers' malintent. In Lön-

---

[61]Ragnars saga loðbrókar 1985, 153. **My translation:** They ask that he identify
himself. He tells them that he is but a single wanderer and that all his life he has
travelled across the lands. "You then should have many tidings to bear, of those things
we would like to know of." The old man replies: "I do not know of which countries
you would like to ask me, that I cannot tell you." "That we want of you, is to tell us
how far from here it is to the city of Rome." He replies: "This I can inform you of the
route. You can see here these iron shoes I have on my feet, they are now ancient, and
this other pair I carry on my back, they are now worn out. When I left from there I tied
the worn out shoes on my feet, those which I now carry on my back, and were both
pairs new at my time of departure, and on this route I have been ever since." And as
the old man had told them of this they felt that this route that they had planned, to the
city of Rome, they could not undertake. And now they turn away with their army and
conquered many cities, which never had been conquered before, and the proof of this
conquest is still visible to this day.

nroth's view this story has an obvious moral to it, "namely that bragging and ostentatious display of wealth is a bad strategy when dealing with ruthless vikings, while the humble appearance of a beggar may be much more efficient in scaring them away. This is a moral that appears very appropriate for pilgrims, and that is probably why the story is associated with the road to Rome in the first place",[62] a view I heartily agree with. The place where the sons of Ragnar loðbrók meet the wanderer, the coastal town of Luna north of Pisa in Italy, incidentally can also be found in Nikulás' Leiðarvísir. Nikulás then reports that, according to hearsay, the sands of Luna contain the snakepit in which Gunnar, another one of the Völsungs, played his harp "svo með mikilli list, að hann drap strengina með tánum og lék svo vel og afbragðlega að fáir þóttust heyrt hafa svo með höndum slegið."[63] His playing was so beautiful that it put all the snakes to sleep and thus kept them from attacking him; that is to say all but one particularly nasty snake which killed him. This scene, along with Sigurður's slaying of Fáfnir, can be found on wooden portals of many early Norwegian stave churches, and in Lönnroth's opinion

> It is obvious that these two scenes are somehow connected
> in religious imagination, and most scholars nowadays
> agree that they must have had some kind of pious signifi-
> cance for the Old Norse congregations of the 12th century.
> According to [...] Klaus Düwel, Sigurd's slaying of Fafnir
> as well as Gunnar's harp-playing in the snakepit may be
> interpreted as typological prefigurations of Christ's vic-

---

[62]Lönnroth, Lars. 1990, 23-4.

[63]Ragnars saga loðbrókar 1985, 90. **My translation:** "with such emotion, that he struck the strings with his toes og played so well and marvelously that few thought they had heard such playing even by hand."

tory over Hell. However that may be, the presence of these mythological scenes in Abbot Nikolás' itinerary should probably be seen as analogous to their presence in the entrance of stave churches: in both cases they serve as a sort of pagan prelude to religious scenes of a higher order, scenes that are more obviously loaded with Christian doctrine.[64]

The last Germanic myth referenced by Nikulás took place in Þiðreksbað, where Þiðrik from Bern was bathing when he saw a hart. Eager to hunt it, he mounts a black horse standing close by and begins pursuit. He then finds out that the horse is in fact a demon, and cries out to his men: "Ek ríð illa [...] þetta mun vera einn fjandi, er ek sit á. En aftr mun ek koma, þá guð vill ok sankta María." Þiðrik was never seen again, but because he remembered God and Mary at the time of his death, he was rewarded by them.[65] This legend, according to Lönnroth, "was often used in Christian teaching and frequently illustrated in the churches of the 12th century as an exemplum, showing how even the highest and mightiest may suddenly be called away from this life and how necessary it consequently is to repent." He further goes on to say:

Also in this case, the Germanic myth turns out to contain a Christian message for the pious pilgrim. And it is a very appropriate message at this particular stage of the journey, just before entering Rome and [having] their sins

---

[64]Lönnroth, Lars. 1990, 28-9

[65]Þiðreks saga af Bern 1962, 438. **My translation:** "This is hardly my doing [...] this must be some devil I sit upon. But I shall be back, when God and Saint Mary so wish it."

redeemed. Needless to say, this is the purpose of a pilgrimage, and all the memorabilia along the road should preferably serve that purpose. The Christian message should be present every time the pilgrim enters a new church, visits a new shrine, admires another relic of some celebrated martyr or father of the church. We may conclude that all of Abbot Nikolás' references to Germanic heroes are also meant to contain such a message. They are intended to lead the pilgrim gradually from the pagan world of Norse myth to the Christian world of God's chosen martyr's [sic], culminating in the holy shrines of Rome and Jerusalem. The Leiðarvísir is thus a travel guide not only in the literal but in the spiritual and theological sense.[66]

This is no coincidence, nor is it an isolated account. In a world view so strongly based in Christian allegory and symbolism, the interpretation and meaning of specific locations is an important and a very much alive part of everyday life. The road to redemption was symbolically and allegorically important, in a cultural, theological and a personal sense, and it was also a path to prestige and enlightenment. The road was, however, filled with dangers not of the orthodox kind to a modern viewer. Dangers that were very much real to the medieval mind which, just as much as anything mentioned above, certainly belonged to the medieval Christian world view.

---

[66]Lönnroth, Lars. 1990, 30-31.

2.3 Medieval travelogues and the mappae mundi

Returning to Dinzelbacher's "fantastic creatures", we must familiarize ourselves with medieval travel narratives and their relation to the medieval world view as portrayed in the mappae mundi, the medieval world maps.

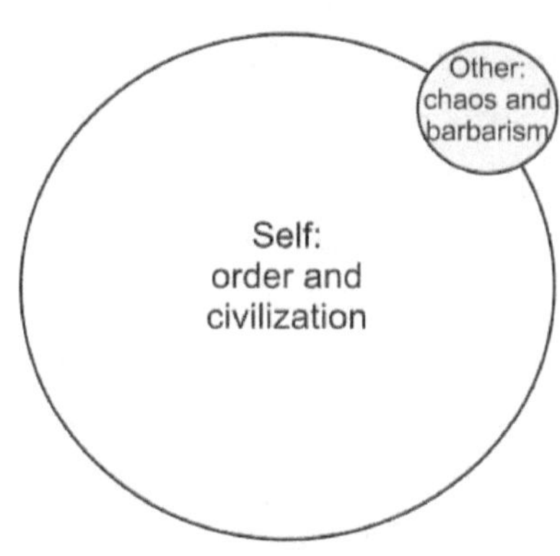

Figure 4: Self and other

As already has been mentioned, a concept deeply rooted in travelogues from the Middle Ages and later times, as well as in other travel narratives that for the sake of genre do not count as travelogues but rather as sagas (such as *Grænlendinga saga* and *Eiríks saga rauða*, and other smaller chapters from various Íslendingasögur), and in the world view itself, is that of 'the other'. The 'otherness' of strange beings and indigenous peoples of far away countries alike furthermore defines their level of supernaturality, as I will explore in full later on. Strange beings are indeed reported in travel narratives from the earliest days of writing[67] up until the 19th century and perhaps even onward.[68] That which is farther

---

[67]E.g. the Sumeran epic of Gilgamesh, Homer's Odysseus and most of the medieval Icelandic travel narratives.

[68]The boundaries themselves are interchanging throughout time, so that monsters typically found on the edge of the known world in the 13th century are much rather to be found on the edge of cultivable farmlands in 19th century folklore, or on or beyond nearby liminal spaces such as forests, mountains and lakes. This can also be seen in travelogues from between the two eras, such as in Reisubók Jóns Indíafara (Jón

away is by definition also increasingly exotic, and in medieval times this meant that the select few explorers who had the chance to travel around the known world in actuality had the last say in what was to be found on the peripheries of the world, and everywhere in between home and there.

I do not mean, however, that they made up the creatures they saw outside the edges of the world; their existence was already very well known to Europeans long before the exploration of the farther world hit medieval pop-culture.[69] It was rather to be expected that such marvelous creatures were lurking in these regions, and the travel narratives met with these expectations. As mentioned earlier, Kirsten Hastrup and Sverrir Jakobsson have convincingly argued for a necessary dichotomy between the *self* and the *other*, a notion which still is very much alive to the modern mind (not least in modern political discourse, from the extremities of fascism to 21st century queer and feminist theory).[70] As is shown in *figure 4*, a designated geographical, cultural and/or ethnic self inevitably brings into being a geographically, culturally and/or ethnic other on the outer rim of the social circle, and that which is outside the normalized self/civilization is inferior, if not monstrous. It is imperative to keep this in mind when dealing with travel narratives, for it lies at the core of the genre itself. In her article, *Boundaries of DiÞerence in the Vínland Sagas*, Williamsen defines the implicit necessity of a functioning travel narrative thusly:

> In order to leave one place and enter another, the traveler
> must cross some sort of border that delineates the home

Ólafsson 1992), where many strange peoples are reported, as well as in parodies of such literature, such as Gulliver's travels to Lilliput, Brobdingnag and the country of the Houyhnhnms among others (Swift 2011).

[69]Reed Kline, Naomi. 2005, 27.

[70]See e.g. Butler 1993.

space from the destination. This border may be a physical boundary, such as a mountain range or an ocean, or it may be an imaginary, constructed boundary of difference that divides the spaces identified as home and non-home [...] All travel narratives are inherently narratives of difference, in that the destination described is not perceived as identical to the homeland – if it were, it would not be a destination. If there exist no physical boundaries to be crossed, then boundaries must be constructed, for without crossing boundaries, the traveler cannot arrive at his destination.[71]

This not only applies to the sagas in her study, i.e. *Grænlendinga saga* and *Eiríks saga rauða*, but to most if not all other Icelandic travel narratives. The boundaries of difference are all at once culturally, religiously and geographically drawn, and Williamsen argues further that although "a medieval travel narrative might indeed be bound by a religious or economic agenda, the text nonetheless presents otherness to the reader [...] The "self" of the travel narrative is removed from its familiar context and placed into strange or even dangerous situations that may call for a rethinking of assumptions, whether about the foreign culture or about its own."[72]

This Christian world view, with its inherent sense of the geographically, culturally, religiously and ethnically 'other', can be clearly viewed on the various mappae mundi that have been preserved through the ages. Here I will mainly focus on the *Hereford mappa mundi*, a medieval map from around 1300, currently on display in the Hereford Cathedral in England.

---

[71] Williamsen, E. A. 2005, 454.
[72] Williamsen, E. A. 2005, 543.

This largest medieval map in known existence follows the classic T-O schema with the East on top, the South to the right, the North on the left and the West at the bottom. Paradise itself nestles in the high East on an impenetrable circular island, above which – outside the corporeal world – the Lord almighty resides. One of the map's most interesting features is how the Mediterranean inter-

Figure 5: T-O map schema

connects with the Black Sea and by geographical error thence north-wards to the Caspian Sea, at the tip of which lies the enclosure that barricades the Antichrist itself from the rest of the world. In a similar spirit, Gog and Magog[73] may be found in Scythia (ca. modern day Siberia). Jerusalem is of course in the center of the world map and Noah's Ark is in place as well. On the extreme peripheries of the North and South, monstrous races may be found.

These sights are not at all uncommon on medieval world maps; in fact, their absence would be highly out of the ordinary. Evelyn Edson has researched a handful of mappae mundi, all containing similar allusions to religious doctrine, most notably Noah's Ark and Gog and Magog along with the regular inclusion of Adam and Eve. To the modern observer, she argues, this may seem to be out of place on a map depicting the 'real', tangible world, "So, are Adam and Eve

---

[73]The ultimate enemies of God's people. Isidore in his Etymologieae (IX, 2.27, 2.89) says that people generally identified them as personifications of the Goths.

40

"imaginary" or "real"?[74] she asks. While the map simultaneously contains real cities, countries and landmarks, it also contains Paradise and Adam and Eve, but this was not a problem for medieval cartographers, as all of this was equally real even though it did not necessarily belong to the same realm:

> The pictorial Palestine maps show Noah's Ark perched on a mountain in Armenia, and the enclosure of Gog and Magog in northern Asia. These savage tribes, identified with the Tartars in Matthew's day, would burst out of their enclosure and ally themselves with the Antichrist in a prelude to the impending last days [...] The historical authenticity of such places may seem dubious to us, but to travelers in the Holy Land – perhaps especially to armchair travelers – they were sites of intense interest [...] Yet, he reminds us that there was not a single model of the map in the Middle Ages, and that medieval mapmakers could entertain multiple visions of the world, emphasizing its different aspects.[75]

Edson's argument is that everything on the mappae mundi is real: "To those who made it, those who commissioned it and those who saw it, it was a true picture of the world" and that the "main question for the mapmaker who would depict the world was, how to represent that greater reality behind the physical appearance."[76]

---

[74]Edson, Evelyn. 2005, 12-13.
[75]Edson, Evelyn. 2005, 15.
[76]Edson, Evelyn. 2005, 17-18.

Figure 6: The antichrist on the Hereford Mappa Mundi

Her conclusion is clearly substantiated by the number of theological authorities found on these maps. Returning to the Hereford map, Christ presides over the world depicted with angels on his right hand leading the virtuous into Paradise, alongside the virgin Mary who pleads for the redemption of the sinners situated on his left hand "who are being quick-marched by devils into the gaping jaws of Hell."[77]

Emperor Augustus is there as well, in the lower left corner, issuing out his census decree of the year 6 CE, and along with it is a quotation from the gospel of Luke authenticating and explaining this. Edson continues: "As if one emperor were not enough, an inscription running around the circle of the map notes that the "orbis terrarum" or circle of lands first began to be surveyed under Julius Caesar. Another inscription attributes the material on the map to the work of Orosius, a fourth-century historian, whose work began with a much-copied geographical chapter. With all these evidences of authority, how can we say the mappamundi is "imaginary"?"[78]

Sverrir Jakobsson is of a different opinion in regard to their importance and points out a central problem with the mappae mundi: that the Earth had in fact been known to be spherical for thousands

---

[77] Edson, Evelyn. 2005, 16.
[78] Edson, Evelyn. 2005, 16-17.

of years before Columbus sailed to America,[79] and that this knowledge was present in Iceland as medieval astrological manuscripts frequently mention that the Earth is a sphere, or „jarðarböllr".[80] This view would be contrary to the concept of „heimskringla", a disc-shaped Earth, a word which nonetheless is also used in books which contain knowledge of a spherical Earth (this knowledge includes facts such as the existence of an Equator, with two equally cold poles to the North and South of its belt). The mappae mundi on the other hand present the viewer with a disc-shaped Earth of a T-O schema where no South hemisphere is to be found, and this is the case with all medieval maps Sverrir states, though this is not entirely true as at least the Walsperger map from 1448 includes Antarctica, as I will come to shortly. Sverrir disagrees with Simek's postulation that these maps were only meant to depict the Northern hemisphere,[81] as that would require the North side to be situated on the middle of the map, and so it would seem that the astronomical knowledge did not necessarily reach the cartographers, whose representation of the world sprung from different ideas. According to Sverrir the maps are of no practical use as medieval people were not used to visual representations of the world's layout,[82] which he bases on the fact that far fewer maps have been preserved than written descriptions of the world.[83]

I will not go so far as to say that I fully disagree with Sverrir on this point; the mappae mundi obviously serve no useful purpose as road maps for instance, but to argue that their part in the medieval world view has been overrated[84] on the basis that countering knowledge

---

[79]Þorsteinn Vilhjálmsson. 1986.

[80]Sverrir Jakobsson. 2010, 232.

[81]Simek, Rudolf. 1992.

[82]Sverrir Jakobsson. 2010, 232-3.

[83]Sverrir Jakobsson. 2005, 83.

[84]This is not to say I cannot agree with Sverrir Jakobsson that perhaps they have

was at the very least accessible, if not common, is in my view only considerable if we see it as paradoxical that these two very different ideas of the physical world existed at the same time. Besides the fact that many medieval sources are paradoxes galore, we may not necessarily know if these discrepansies were considered paradoxical in the Middle Ages. Christianity, as with other religions, is in many ways inconsistent,[85] and so are our sources on Old Norse mythology.[86]

---

been overrated in some respects, e.g. the idea that Snorri Sturluson based the Prologus of Heimskringla on a mappa mundi (Sverrir Tómasson. 2001, 25), for which we have absolutely no evidence nor any particular reason to believe.

[85] As Schjødt, Jens Peter 2007, 49. put it: "Sådan er det bare ikke. Tilsyneladende lever de fleste mennesker udmærket, selv om deres religiøse anskuelser ind i mellem er aldeles usammenhængende. Deres guder er både i templet og i himlen, de er både antropomorfe og ikke-antropomorfe. De døde er i et paradis, men får alligevel gaver med i graven. Ritualerne indebærer, at man æder guden, men det er alligevel ikke rigtigt guden, osv. I de såkaldte højreligioner betragtes den slags som mysterier, og så er det ikke så galt, som når de primitive har lignende usammenhængende op-fattelser; men hvis man er tilstrækkelig udviklet, bør tingene hænge sammen uden selvmodsigelser. Og det er da også den måde, den videnskabelige erkendelse med nødvendighed må fungere på; men religion er ikke videnskab og er måske netop karakteriseret ved denne forskel i forhold til den videnskabelige tænkning. Medens den logik, der nemlig karakteriserer den videnskabelige tænkning, er en formallogik, er den religiøse tænkning kendetegnet ved en konkret logik, som gælder inden for bestemte mentale rum, men ikke er beregnet på at være modsigelsesfri i forhold til andre mentale rum. Det indebærer, at en gud fx kan være karakteriseret på én måde i én myte, og anderledes i en anden, og undertiden vil de to karakteristikker være i direkte modstrid med hinanden. Men det betyder omvendt ikke, at alt kan siges om denne gud."

[86] Cf. Simek, Rudolf. 1993, 111; Schjødt, Jens Peter 2007, 38-9. Also of note is the difference between Saxo Grammaticus' Gesta Danorum and Snorri Sturluson's Edda, e.g. the myth of the death of Baldur (Gesta Danorum 2000, 107-117.); (Snorra-Edda 2002, 62-65.). Snorri may have based his version on Völuspá (Eddukvæði 1998, 10-11.). Again, we can note the difference between Snorra Edda and Snorri's Heimskringla, which is a subject of debate yet is not considered paradoxical (see e.g. Nordvig, Mathias. 2011, 20.). In contrast, Boulhosa views that Snorri's authorship of Heimskringla is based

Yet we do not consider these discrepancies to be paradoxes, as they most certainly existed at the same time then as they still do.[87]

There may also be other reasons for why the mappae mundi contradict contemporary astronomical knowledge, reasons as simple as whether cartographers even *could* show a spherical Earth in a period when all drawings were two dimensional and disproportionate. The mappae mundi did not have to be realistic, they just had to represent the continents "sort of" as they lay, and if such visual representations of the world were outside the scope of the common medieval mind then the maps must on the contrary to Sverrir's argument have been applicable enough for convincing people that they indeed *were* a realistic depiction of the world. After all, how could anyone say different?

Medieval maps were not a reliable source on the layout of Earth's realms, for sure, but they certainly did, as they were indubitably meant to, portray the world allegorically, i.e. from a theological point of view. It need not be said that, to the medieval mind, Hell, Purgatory and Paradise were factual places, the last of which was geographically placed on Earth on mappae mundi;[88] the topmost level of Hell, on

---

on conjectural evidence at best (Boulhosa, Patricia Pires. 2005, 6-21.), which would eliminate the problem if proven.

[87]Here I am not only referring to the extant religious sources, but societies based around world views profoundly contrary to modern knowledge. The Flat Earth Society, for one, is not a parody as it would seem, but a genuine group of believers of the idea that the Earth is an oblate spheroid. Their webpage is to be found at: *http://theflatearthsociety.org/cms/*

[88]It is well clear in the *Biblia Vulgata* that Paradise is on Earth. Four rivers water Paradise: Phison, Gehon, Tigris and Euphrates (Gen. 2:10-14). The last two are in Mesopotamia, which fits with the location of Paradise on mappae mundi. When Adam and Eve are cast from Paradise, God places cherubim and a flaming sword in front of the gate so that no one may enter again (Gen. 3:24). Not surprisingly in this context, the word 'paradise' comes from ancient Persian 'pairidaêza', meaning 'walled garden' (Ásgeir Blöndal Magnússon. 1989, 701.).

the other hand, was the lowest part of this world according to the *Elucidarius*, and the lower Hell was "under the Earth".[89] Based on this, Sverrir Tómasson presumes that visionary literature was in a way realistic literature in the minds of people in the Middle Ages. Learned men seemed to be in agreement on where Paradise on Earth was to be found; Isidore of Sevilla places it in the East,[90] Hrabanus Maurus and Honorius Augustodunensis agree, the latter stating that Paradise is "Inn fegursti staður í austri".[91] This learned geography is more meticulous in the manuscripts AM 194 8vo and Hauksbók, according to Sverrir Tómasson, which themselves are based on learned lore and oral accounts.[92]

To return then to Edson's argument, in accepting it we admit that the purpose of the mappae mundi is to not only convey the physical world, but also the "greater reality behind the physical appearance."[93] This is a plausible explanation, yet it leaves us with the fact that there are still monsters roaming about the world, in particular in Scythia and in Africa, i.e. the farthest regions to the North and to the South, which again leaves us with the question of whether the maps can be considered "real" or not. When considering the possible reality of monsters, the truth may not always be obvious even by modern standards, but putting them down as landmarks on a map most certainly seems absurd to the modern viewer.

John Block Friedman has observed that in the Middle Ages, mild

---

[89]Elucidarius 1989, 102. **Icelandic:** Ið efra helvíti er hinn neðsti hlutur þessa heims [...] Hið neðra helvíti er andleg kvöl, það er óslökkvilegur eldur, sem ritað er: Þú leystir önd mína frá helvíti hinu neðra (SI 86:13). Sá staður er undir jörðu, að svo sé andir syndugar grafnar í píslir sem líkamir í jörð.

[90]In Etymologiae 1911: xiv. 3,2 (according to Sverrir Tómasson. 2001, 28.)

[91]Elucidarius 1989, 57. **My translation:** The most beautiful place in the East.

[92]Sverrir Tómasson. 2001, 28.

[93]Edson, Evelyn. 2005, 18.

climates where thought to produce "moral" people, while more harsh climates were thought to produce the opposite. According to Friedman, these milder climates resembled that of Eden, and by association the perfection of the creation of God, namely Adam,[94] but the farther from the center of the world[95] the less godly the climate was, and as were the people – by geographical association. On the world's peripheries the weather was extremely hot or extremely cold, and such a climate produced monstrous races "whose physical and moral character show defect from or excess beyond the Aristotelian mean."[96] To the same effect, Naomi Reed Kline points again to the Hereford map and its description of the inhabitants of Scythia, which is by far the most damning of all, describing horrific cannibalistic peoples among other things:

> Scythia is shown to be particularly fraught with dangers, especially the 'enclosure' of the Antichrist that occupies a substantial portion of the geography of Scythia. The place is enclosed on three sides by mountains. The fourth side is surmounted by four tower-like structures or castellations. The accompanying texts suggest a Christian conflation of material taken from the Alexander legend and Solinus. The place is described as 'more horrible than is able to be believed; intolerably cooled in every season by the fiercest wind from the mountains which the inhabitants call the Northeast wind (Bizo). The northern realms are thus associated with darkness and evil. 'Here there are very savage

---

[94]It goes without saying that Eve, of course, was not considered to be 'as perfect' as Adam.

[95]Or the narrative middle, as discussed earlier.

[96]Friedman, John Block. 2005, 53.

men feeding on human flesh, drinking blood . . . ' [. . .] In this case the enclosing wall is not a safe haven but rather a tenuous container of the forces of evil. It is the monstrous counterpart to the Garden of Eden and Jerusalem."[97]

Figure 7: Pictured, among others, a sciopod (far left) and a blemmye (second from the right).

The aforementioned Walsperger map is considered one of the most modern for its time, showing knowledge of the latest Ptolemaic ideas and fixing various geographical misconceptions. On it, Christian cities are marked with red dots, whereas Muslim cities are marked with black dots – which in itself is interesting, yet perhaps hard to deduct any truth from. This map also contains the monstrous. Gog and Magog are there behind Alexander the Great's enclosure. A race of giants can be found in Patagonia. The supremely monstrous races have been displaced however and moved to the Antarctic, and are said to be the most marvelous monsters, not only among animals, but even among men. To name a few, there are cyclopes, blemmyae (men with no heads but faces on their chests instead), troglodytes (a primitive three-faced race) and sciopods (unipeds). "In sum, Walsperger presents a goodly number

[97] Reed Kline, Naomi. 2005, 37-8.

of the traditional monstrous races, not in their usual lands of India or Africa, but at the South Pole."[98]

We have now established some rudimentary rules by which monsters and monstrous races are depicted and placed on the world map – but did they certainly belong to the world view? As Reed Kline has pointed out, distant races and strange peoples garnered great interest and popularity among Europeans, from stories such as the travel narratives previously mentioned. And indeed this interest was taken seriously, perhaps not least of all for the reason that the information on these strange folk was of unverifiable veracity: "The various ways in which this material was disseminated in the Middle Ages present us with a glimpse of reconciling strange races, largely known through antique sources, was to be tenuously reconciled within the historical and Christian context of the Middle Ages."[99] In fact, the existence of monsters was taken so seriously that:

> The debate regarding the question of redemption for human monstrosities had a long history. In the Middle Ages, scholars referred to St. Augustine's Civitas Dei for guidance in dealing with the predicament that monsters posed for the Church. Expanding upon such treatieses as Isidore of Seville's discussion of monstrous races, Augustine grappled with the question of how the Church could reconcile the presence of monstrous races with a world of God's creation. To begin, Augustine described monsters as prodigies, placed on this earth as indication of God's power to create all things.[100]

---

[98] Friedman, John Block. 2005, 47-8.
[99] Reed Kline, Naomi. 2005, 27.
[100] Reed Kline, Naomi. 2005, 27.

The monsters' alleged existence was thus interpreted as a proof of
God's plan and final judgement, serving their own purpose within
the higher divine order of things. And as for the notion of the 'other',
"... many Christians still believed that monsters represented the
'other', a world of portents unknown [...] their deformed characteristics were believed to be signs of God's displeasure, corroborated by
crusading literature that was replete with evidence of projection of
monstrous traits upon the enemy. The Hereford Mappamundi [...]
provides us with a visual attempt to reconcile these two opposing
viewpoints."[101] The German Catholic scholar Konrad von Megenberg
was also concerned with monstrous races when he around 1350 wrote
the following:

> nu sprich ich Megenbergær, daz die wundermenschen
> zwaierlai sint: etleich sint gesêlet und etleich niht. die
> gesêlten wundermenschen haiz ich die ain menschleich
> sêl habent und die doch geprechen habent. die ungesêl-
> ten haiz ich die etswaz ain menschleich gestalt habent an
> dem leib und doch kain menschleich sêl habent. die gesêl-
> ten wundermenschen sint auch zwaierlai. etleich habent
> geprechen an dem leib und etleich an der sêl werk, und
> die koment paideu von Adam und von seinen sünden,
> wan ich glaub daz: hiet der êrst mensch niht gesünt, all
> menschen wæren ân geprechen geporn.[102]

---

[101] Reed Kline, Naomi. 2005, 28.

[102] Konrad von Megenberg, Buch der Natur, ca. 1349. Rudolf Simek supplied me
with this information, much to my gratitude. Regretfully I cannot produce the proper
citation for this quote at present. Simek was kind enough to provide me with a rough
translation as well:

"monsters are 2fold, some with soul, some without, The ones with a soul I call
human, despite being handcapped, the ones without soul may have traces of human

It is thus evident that the monstrous was of concern to the clergy and was accepted into Christian doctrine on the basis of that concern. The conception of the world as represented by these monstrous races most undoubtedly found its way to Iceland, just as the religion and its implicit world view did, and the evidence of the knowledge of this monstrous geography is widespread within medieval Icelandic literature.

appearance, but no soul. The ones with soul also are 2fold: some handicapped in body, others in soul, but both stem from Adam and his sins, because I believe that if Adam hadn't sinned, all people would be born without handcap."

2.4 Medieval Icelandic literature as part of a Christian world view

Let us again look at the arguments produced so far:

1. There is a sense of 'otherness' present in travel narratives from ancient to modern times. The self cannot exist without the other.

2. This seems to be equally true in the case of visionary travels and pilgrimages. Travels were important both from a material and a spiritual point of view. Imbued in the world view was a theological, allegorical meaning of a heavenly world order and a holy code of moral. The 'other' in this context is the godless, he who strays from the path of God; the 'self' being the pious, selfless Christian.

3. The monstrous, a definite other, was an integral part of this world view, depicted on world maps as being a factual part of the divine order by various theological authorities, and described in travelogues and other contemporary narratives as strange and undesirable races, stories of whom gained immense popular interest.

4. In an attempt to reconcile the existence of these monstrous beings, they were adopted into Christian canon by no lesser prophets than Isidore of Seville and St. Augustine. In every respect, the monstrous thus undoubtedly belonged to the medieval Christian world view.

Returning to Icelandic literature, let us quickly look at two travel narratives in light of our findings so far. Yngvar víðförli travels to Austrvegr (between modern day Finland and Russia). On their way

there, he and his companions encounter fearsome dragons. Then
they arrive at the city Citópólis, which is full of paganry, yet they
hold firmly to their Christian faith. Upon further travels they come
across more pagans and battle with many giants and dragons. The
names of the various cities they find along their way indicates "some
knowledge of clerical authorities, such as the Bible and Isidore of
Seville," according to Sverrir Jakobsson,[103] and he goes on to say that:

> Encounters with giants and dragons typify the nature of
> the lands visited by Yngvar. These creatures belong to
> the realm of the unknown and fantastic. However, such
> encounters are hardly exclusive to the East. Treasures,
> giants and dragons could be found in any unknown lands,
> not only those belonging to the East.[104]

I agree with Sverrir on all points except that I disagree with the claim
that the creatures he mentions belong to "the realm of the unknown
and fantastic". While this is an accepted usage of the term *fantastic*, bearing in mind the existence of stranger beings within Christian
doctrine, such as the sciopods or the blemmyae, creatures that most
certainly were considered real at this time in European history, I find
the argument for the fantastic nature of the creatures Yngvar meets
naught but unconvincing from an historical point of view. The monsters themselves are not to be taken lightly as they still roamed the
lands outside of literature, in very much the same way we can still
believe that certain animals exist, even if within e.g. a cartoon or a
comic book they possess abilities not naturally possible to the species:
even though Donald Duck drives a car in a cartoon we do not doubt
the existence of ducks.

---

[103]Sverrir Jakobsson. 2006, 940.
[104]Sverrir Jakobsson. 2006, 940.

The travels of Yngvar's son Sveinn, incidentally, are also characterized by an abundance of "wondrous beasts, fighting with pagans, and
the spreading of the Christian faith to the lands of Silkisif", whereas
in Eiríks saga víðförla:

> there is no mention of dragons or giants or other fantastic
> creatures. The East seems very safe and civilized, and no
> heathen armies make the journey to Paradise hazardous
> for the protagonist and his fellowship. It seems that this
> description mostly serves to emphasize the glory of the
> emperor and his authority in distant lands. The lands on
> the way to Paradise do not seem to merit any mention until
> the companions approach the river Phison (the modern
> Ganges), which was thought to originate in Paradise.[105]

Eiríkur follows this river to the farthest east, to the gates of Paradise,
but cannot enter because it is protected by a fiery wall. In spite of
the lack of wondrous beasts on his way, the Garden of Eden is in its
place according to contemporary world view. There is nothing out
of the ordinary for the learned or the lay in any of these narratives,
for these occurences were exactly what one would have expected at
the time. The connection between the medieval Christian world view
and medieval Icelandic travelogues is indisputable. What, then, can
be said of Íslendingasögur?

---

[105]Sverrir Jakobsson. 2006, 940-41.

3. The monstrous and the supernatural in Íslendingasögur

3.1 Previous research

Over 22 years ago, Torfi Tulinius presented a unique paper on geography and the categorization of saga literature. The idea is that with change of setting in a saga, the laws of narrative may change in accordance with the geographical location.

He names two very specific examples in support of his hypothesis, which in itself need not be as specific as the principle can work on a lot subtler scale; these examples are *Samsons saga*, an indigenous Icelandic Riddarasaga (Knight's Tale) – i.e. not translated as most of them were – and *Víglundar saga*, a borderline Íslendingasaga with the structure of a romance.

Samsons saga is preserved in 15th century manuscripts but is considered to have been written in the first half of the 14th century. The saga is about the loves of Samson the fair Artússon[106] and Valentína. Lions however lie in the path of their love and their main antagonist is Kvintalín kvennaþjófur (the stealer of women), but he fails in kidnapping Valentína, gets arrested, and the couple gets married in the end. To save his life, Kvintalín must take on a mission to a far away land in the North to obtain a rare item. Torfi points out that as soon as Kvintalín gets there, the narrative completely changes: the narrative, which originally revolves around French courtship and Celtic wonders, with main characters such as Valentína and Ólympía, completely mutates to Nordic barbarism and trolldom and the reader is

---

[106]That Samson is the son of Artús borders on being a slapstick reference to King Arthur and the knights of the round table.

introduced to characters called Krókur, Krekla and Skrímnir:

Það er einmitt vegna þess að höfundur Samsons sögu heldur efni fornaldarsögunnar og efni riddarasögunnar svo
vandlega aðskildu, með því að binda það við sitthvort sö-
gusviðið, [...] Það er engin tilviljun að aðeins Kvintalín
og aðstoðarmaður hans, dvergurinn Grélant, geta ferðast
úr heimi riddarasögunnar norður á slóðir fornaldarsag-
nanna. Það tengist ólíkum hlutverkum heimanna tveg-
gja í sögunni. Höfundur leggur mikla áherslu á að gera
frásögn sína af tröllabyggðum norðursins eins gróteska og
mögulegt er.[107]

The role of this grotesque realm in the North is to serve as a comic
counterpart to the chivalric realm in the South, as is evident from the
hilarious names of the characters alone.

Víglundar saga is a different example, in which the plot is mostly
borrowed from two Fornaldarsögur, *Þorsteins saga Víkingssonar* and
Friðþjófs saga frœkna: two brothers do not want their sister to marry
the man she loves, he then has to fight the brothers and kill them
before winning her once more. It is also a different example for in
this case the narrative form of a romance has been transported to a
new setting. To disguise the story as an Íslendingasaga, the author
simply added to it various stylistic themes of the intended genre.
The setting is medieval Iceland in the days of Haraldr hárfagri. The
saga also shows a different, more realistic from a medieval point of
view, attitude towards supernatural occurences than Fornaldarsögur
do. The reason this ploy does not work is that the saga breaks the
laws of Íslendingasögur, specifically the law of vengeance: Víglun-

---

[107]Torfi H. Tulinius. 1990, 148.

dur, the protagonist, kills Ketilríður's brothers, yet marries her with her father's blessing, which simply does not make sense within the narrative form of the genre.[108]

Torfi's conclusion is twofold, of which only the first is relevant in this context: geography serves the purpose of opening windows into different saga universes. By transporting a person from an Íslendingasaga to a country connected with heroic tales in the minds of the audience, the author creates tension between the protagonist's possible fate in the "possible world" of the heroic tale and his "real" fate in the Íslendingasaga.[109] This is important, as it may in some ways figure into the various scenes from Íslendingasögur which present the bulk of this thesis. I will not exclude the possibility that, if we choose to only regard the sources as literature, tales from abroad are meant to show alternative possibilities to the realism of the Íslendingasaga. From an historical or a religious perspective however, this need not be the more plausible explanation.

The corpus of research on the supernatural in Old Norse literature is close to overwhelmingly immense, yet, however curiously, most of it is relevant only to the genre of Fornaldarsögur, sometimes stretching thenceforth out to younger recorded Nordic folklore. Little research has been done on the ramifications of beings, who by modern standards would be considered supernatural, being included in the semi-realistic Íslendingasögur. Even fewer attempts have been made to classify the various types of supernatural and/or fantastic creatures,[110] which in my view is essential to understanding their

---

[108]Torfi H. Tulinius. 1990, 149-50, 154.

[109]Torfi H. Tulinius. 1990, 155.

[110]Most notably Ármann Jakobsson. 1998, Ármann Jakobsson. 2006, Ármann Jakobsson. 2008a, Ármann Jakobsson. 2008b, Ármann Jakobsson. 2008c, Ármann Jakobsson. 2009b, Ármann Jakobsson. 2009a, Ármann Jakobsson. 2010, Mundal, Else

inclusion in the literature and behaviour therein.

Classification does not come easy however. I agree with Else Mundal's argument that the distinction between the supernatural and the fantastic is somewhat blurred, and that it is problematic to say the least to distinguish between a supernatural being and a fantastic being. On grounds of this she chooses to:

> discuss both the supernatural and the fantastic as phenom-ena opposed to the real or natural [...] The supernatural deals, according to the standard definitions in dictionaries, with beings and phenomena that are not subject to natural laws The fantastic, on the other hand, deals with beings and phenomena that do not belong to the real, experienced world, but rather to imagination and fantasy.[111]

I believe that this is the right approach.

She then argues that the distinction between the supernatural and the fantastic is important in principle as they have different relations to truth, yet that what could be regarded as truth in that respect is in many cases unclear as it is dependent on many different factors. To clearly define trolls or giants as supernatural or fantastic beings, to name an example, could be difficult.[112] Trolls or giants could perhaps be regarded as supernatural if they are of the mythic kind[113] whereas their more fairytale type namesakes[114] would rather be considered fantastic. In Mundal's view this demarcation problem applies to

2006, Sävborg, Daniel. 2009, Sävborg, Daniel. 2012, Torfi H. Tulinius. 1999, Mitchell, Stephen A. 2009, Mitchell, Stephen A. 2011,

[111]Mundal, Else 2006, 1.

[112]A tröll, after all, is not always the same as a tröll. Cf. Ármann Jakobsson. 2008a, Ármann Jakobsson. 2009b,

[113]This for example may to some degree apply to Bárðr Snæfellsás.

[114]Here I refer to tröll who seem to have some relation to mythological jötnar or

dragons as well, as there "can be little doubt that dragons found in the legends of the Church (in heilagra manna sögur) are supernatural beings since they are representations of the Devil", but that the dragon which "Björn hítdœlakappi has to fight in Bjarnar saga (ch. 5) is, on the other hand, more of the fairy-tale type and belongs to the fantastic world." The majority of the dragons in Fornaldarsögur belong to the fantastic world, but "[on] the basis of the dragon motif alone it is, however, very difficult, if not impossible, to distinguish between the supernatural dragon and the fantastic dragon."[115] And that:

> In other cases it may be easier to label a motif as fantastic. The story about the creature with only one leg, the einfœtingr, in Eiríks saga rauða (ch.12), for instance, is probably a figment of imagination placed in the periphery of the world (in Vínland) without any basis in Old Norse beliefs. Talking animals or birds seem also to belong to the fantastic. There are, however, also animals found in so-called realistic literature which come close to these fantastic creatures, for instance the dog Saur, in Hákonar saga góða in Heimskringla, which the people of Trøndelag chose for their king. By means of sorcery they had put into the dog the understanding of three men, and the dog barked twice but spoke every third word. The fact that this fantastic dog is embedded in a realistic saga and is the result of magic, in which people believed, makes the borderline between the supernatural and the fantastic very blurred [...] If we use credibility as a criterion to distinguish between the

þursar. As complicated as it is to confidently reach a conclusion this might possibly be applicable to the jötunn Brúsi in Orms þáttr Stórólfssonar.

[115]Mundal, Else 2006, 1.

supernatural and the fantastic we see again that there is
no sharp line of demarcation between the two.[116]

It seems to me that the fact that the demarcation between the terms
the fantastic and *the supernatural* is unclear indicates not a problem
with how we use them but rather that something is wrong with the
terminology. This problem is in fact inherent in Todorov's popular
definition of the fantastic: "The fantastic is that hesitation experienced
by a person who knows only the laws of nature, confronting an apparently supernatural event."[117] The line of demarcation is "fuzzy" as
Else Mundal put it, not least because Todorov did not himself create
any line of demarcation between the two terms. The fantastic term is
therefore not applicable to medieval literature unless we re-define it.

But why should we? To me it seems this sort of demarcation is
not wholly necessary. I do not agree with Mundal that the distinction
between the supernatural and the fantastic is at all as important as
she suggests, not only because the definition itself is flawed, but for
the simple reason that this method of definiton seems to me to inadvertently overshadow more important elements that need careful
consideration. The fantastic, as opposed to the supernatural, is as
Mundal herself argues indeed in many cases blurred beyond recog-
nition, so much so that in my opinion it may in all too many cases be
beyond reasonable usage within the genre of Íslendingasögur.[118]

---

[116]Mundal, Else 2006, 1-2.

[117]Todorov, Tzvetan. 1975, 25. See also Torfi H. Tulinius. 1999, 290.

[118]It seems to me that (Vésteinn Ólason. 2007) does not make a clear distinction
between the supernatural and the fantastic either, but uses them even-handedly as
they apply to „bæði það sem er yfirnáttúrlegt og stórkostlegar ýkjur" (22). Mundal
uses the term differently as I have already discussed, and (Mitchell, Stephen A. 2009)
and (Torfi H. Tulinius. 1999) both use it in their own way. (Dinzelbacher, Peter. 2005)
mentions the fantastic while discussing the monstrous geography of the Middle Ages,

Mundal also mentions credibility as a criterion for telling the supernatural apart from the fantastic. Mitchell mentions this too, but asks the important question whether the term adequately reflects the reality of medieval people.[119] I for one believe it is a bad criterion. Elementary to the question of 'belief' in phenomena associated with the supernatural/fantastic demarcation is the inevitable disappointment that in many cases we may never know for sure what people actually did or could believe in. When Mundal claims that "we can observe a gradual transition between fantastic motifs describing events which probably nobody would believe had actually taken place – at least not in their own time and within their own environment – and motifs describing events and phenomena which were deeply rooted in people's religious conceptions",[120] she makes an assumption as to what people in the Middle Ages could or could not have believed in, yet we have much evidence to the contrary that beliefs in both supernatural and so-called fantastic phenomena were widespread in Iceland (and elsewhere) from its settlement and well into the 20th century.[121] The

---

but does not further explain what he is referring to. (Sverrir Jakobsson. 2006) mentions that risar and drekar were common in uncharted territories and that they belong to "the realm of the unknown and the fantastic" (940), but like Dinzelbacher he does not further elaborate upon his usage of the term. (Leslie, Helen F. 2009) discusses both "fantastic occurences" and "supernatural beings" in a general way but does not give examples (119) though it seems to me that it must refer to what (Power, Rosemary. 1985) calls "mythological" (156), but in other respects she makes little distinction between the supernatural, fantastic and the fairytale like (Märchen). This chaotic usage of the term 'fantastic' seems to me to indicate that the term is less useful than it is harmful.

[119]Mitchell, Stephen A. 2009, 282.

[120]Mundal, Else 2006, 2.

[121]For late medieval sources (as far as Iceland goes, and to the degree we can consider history as a series of eras rather than a continuous evolutionary period, I subscribe to the definition put forth by Le Goff, Jacques. 2005, of the Middle Ages reaching into the 18th century), cf. e.g. Ólína Þorvarðardóttir 2000, Jón Ólafsson 1992, Jón Árnason.

reason for this is that the demarcation supernatural/fantastic simply did not exist in the Middle Ages.

We do not really know but to a small degree what pre-Christian religious conceptions were like, so in the case of sorcery, shapeshifting and so forth we cannot automatically assume that these phenomena have more to do with the fantastic than they have with actual belief.[122] We also need to bear in mind that the distinction between religion and belief is in many cases an equally ambiguous one as the distinction between the supernatural and the fantastic. For example, the existence of draugar has always been denounced by Christian institutes, yet they were obviously believed in as they still are to some degree; in contrast the existence of magic was widely known and believed in within Christian Europe, as is clearly seen in the various witch trials in Scandinavia[123] and elsewhere, not forgetting the most notable believer in the dark arts in Iceland, the 17th century priest Jón Magnússon, who in his famous, aptly named passio *Píslarsaga* documented his ordeal at the hands of what he believed to be practicioners of black magic. The difference between the two is that the existence of draugar was rejected by the church whereas the existence and execution of witches was sanctioned by it, yet both were equally believed in.

This contrast, in Mundal's opinion, is precisely why the distinction between the supernatural and the fantastic is so important,[124] whereas

---

2003.

[122]In fact the concensus shared by scholars that these phenomena have basis in pagan and/or folk belief is absolute, so it is hard to understand how they could be connected with fantasy at the same time. Cf. Kjartan G. Ottósson. 1983, Gurevich, Aron. 1988, Ármann Jakobsson. 1998, Vésteinn Ólason. 1999, Gunnell, Terry 2002, Torfi H. Tulinius. 2008, Schjødt, Jens Peter. 2009, Sävborg, Daniel. 2009, Sävborg, Daniel. 2012, Jón Ma. Ásgeirsson. 2009, Mitchell, Stephen A. 2011,

[123]E.g. Mitchell, Stephen A. 1998, Árni Magnússon 1962,

[124]Mundal, Else 2006, 3-4.

I would argue the opposite for the very same reason. Magic does not seem more fantastic than draugar in this context. If it was, and if pre-Christians and Christians alike would not believe in sorcery, supernatura, or the existence of monsters, we would be forced to assume that the events described in *Biskupasögur*, *Heilagra manna sögur* and other hagiographic texts were not something Christians could actually believe in either, yet nothing seems to indicate this.[125] As Le Goff has pointed out, medieval scholars had three categories for these phenomena: *miraculosa*, *magica* and *mirabilia*. The first two categories belong to the Christian world view; miracula are acts of God and magica are acts of the Devil.[126] That which belongs in neither group was called mirabilia and many supernatural phenomena connected to folk belief and paganism belong to that category. The problem in explaining phenomena represented by mirabilia, and finding them a place within the twofold Christian world view in this case, is what Todorov referred to as the fantastic, it is what cannot clearly separate good and evil,[127] which has no tangible connection with mythological beings such as the dragons of the Fornaldarsögur. This is explained in Dubost's model (*figure 8*).[128]

---

[125]Hagiographic stories had hardly been written and told if they were not considered to have an effect on their recipients. See especially Gurevich, Aron. 1988, 1-8.

[126]More on this in Mitchell, Stephen A. 2009, 285-6.

[127]Cf. Torfi H. Tulinius. 1990, 291.

[128]Recreated from Torfi H. Tulinius. 1999,

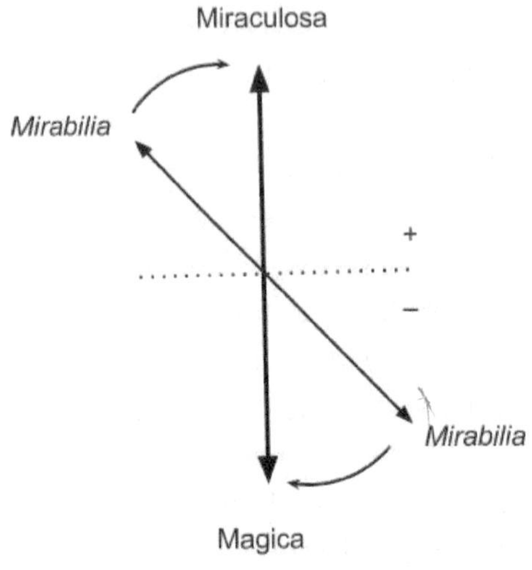

Figure 8: Dubost's model

The arced arrows show the tension from the tendency to define strange phenomena with the plus-minus system of Christianity. The uncertainty with how to categorize the supernatural creates this tension, but attempts at defining the undefined marvels of the world are at the same time an opportunity to solve the mystery of the self.[129] The other cannot exist without the self, as I mentioned before.

Even if for some reason we were to reject this we would be forgetting loads of carefully documented folklore from later ages, not least from Iceland, and the widespread belief in e.g. *álfar, huldufólk* and other supernatural beings that Icelanders have thought to exist through the ages and into the 21st century.[130] An example of this is the six volume collection of Icelandic folklore *Íslenskar þjóðsögur og ævintýri*, collected by Jón Árnason in the 19th century, which is testament to the general belief in supernatural beings and occurrences,

---

[129]Cf. Torfi H. Tulinius. 1999, 292.

[130]Cf. Unnur Jökulsdóttir. 2007. Such beliefs are however not common anymore and have been parodied, e.g. in Hallgerður Hallgrímsdóttir. 2005.

most of which, if not all, have roots in ancient folk belief.[131] An orally transmitted story describing supernatural phenomena occurring in other people's lives are indeed something medieval people would have believed in, even more so the further they were removed from the person in question, how much time had elapsed since the events took place, etc.

In other words: I do not think that credibility is a reasonable criterion for estimating the veracity medieval narratives had in the minds of their audience,[132] as Mundal admits could be complicated,[133] and I see no indication that the term *fantastic* is by any means applicable within this field of research; to use it is to analyse a perceived reality with a term denoting fiction. A dragon in a medieval text is, in other words, a dragon, and nothing within medieval Icelandic literature indicates that a dragon may be considered to be fantastic, whether

---

[131] Gunnell, Terry 2002, 191-197.

[132] This may seem like a strange comparison to some readers, but I would like to name the American television program *Scare Tactics* as an example of what even educated modern people can believe in. It is comfortable to sit at home and laugh when an enormous alien monster tears the door off a car close to Roswell, New Mexico, as such things only happen in movies, but the person sitting trapped in the back seat is by no means amused is he thinks that exactly this is happening to him in reality. Where the boundaries of the believable lie is therefore a valid question, not less whether we are in a position to judge where they lay in the Middle Ages.

[133] "The belief that certain beings really existed, even though few, if any, people had seen them, and that strange things caused by magic or sorcery could happen is, as I see it, the main criterion for distinguishing between the supernatural and the fantastic. However, there is no sharp division between the believable and the unbelievable. It is no doubt true that fantastic – and supernatural – elements are much more frequent in texts which tell about events that happened long ago and far away than in stories from the author's own time and environment. The explanation for this, that people were more willing to believe that strange things could happen in the distant past and in foreign countries than in their own time and milieu, may be true – to some extent." Mundal, Else 2006, 3.

within historical accounts or as a literary motif.

3.2 Mode of analysis

Based on this reasoning, I will suggest a system of classification of the supernatural, barring the term 'fantastic' altogether.

As I mentioned in the introduction to this thesis, I have classified three types of uncanny beings on which I will base my analysis.[134] Each of these types works more or less by the same narrative principle within the Íslendingasögur. They share common characteristics and follow a set of preliminary rules which admittedly are sometimes broken and sometimes bent around their role within the narrative. The three classes of uncanny beings analyzed in this research are, along with their synonyms and/or subcategories:

1. Draugar: *afturganga, haugbúi*

2. Tröll: *þurs, jötunn, skessa, gýgur, risi, skrælingi, blámaður, ketta*

3. Ófreskjur: *dreki, flugdreki, finngálkn*

These categories are of course neither sacred nor absolute, as some of the subcategorized beings belong in between categories or in two adjacent categories. Á blámaðr can for example be more like a finngálkn in his general behaviour, save for his ambiguous nature as a human being.[135]

---

[134]There are of course more, but for the sake of brevity I have simplified the selection.

[135]On the ambiguous nature of tröll, cf. Ármann Jakobsson. 2006, Ármann Jakobsson. 2008a, Ármann Jakobsson. 2009b,

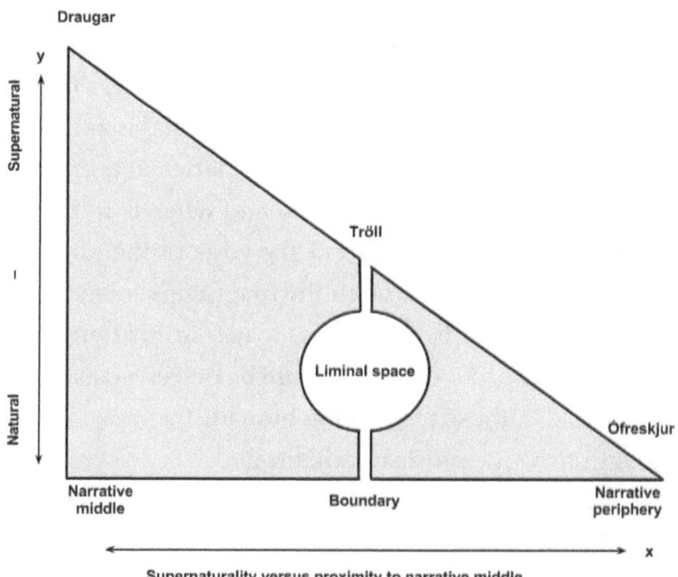

If we return now to the thesis model, the common characteristics each group shares is that of the *boundary* the protagonist must cross to encounter a being from each group respectively; their *proximity to the narrative middle*, i.e. where geographically the protagonist would come across them; and their *level of supernaturality*, which is directly linked with how common or uncommon the being is and how believable or unbelievable it would be to encounter them. Based on the saga material presented later in this paper, one might depict the perfect distinction between these groups, if a perfect one could be made, as I have done in the above visual representation.

For convenience I have marked in standard *x* and *y* axes. The *x* axis describes each group's proximity to the narrative middle, ranging from the narrative middle to the narrative periphery with a boundary in between them. The model assumes that draugar mostly, if not always, come creeping around the narrative middle. Tröll tend to inhabit mountains or other hard to reach places and in fact seem most of the time to dwell within or on the boundaries of a liminal space. Ófreskjur are what one would expect to find when that liminal space has been crossed, i.e. on or beyond the edge of the known world. The diagonal line running through the diagram is intended to show each type's relationship to the y axis, which in turn describes how supernatural the respective beings would be perceived as being in the eye of the beholder, those resembling humans the most, i.e. draugar, being thought to be the most supernatural.

First, I will make an attempt at creating clearer definitions for each group based on the hypothesis using examples to support my case. I will then examine each encounter in each saga respectively as an isolated event using the set of properties that follow from the hypothesis, i.e.: 1) does the encounter take place within the narrative middle, the narrative periphery, or on or around the liminal space dividing them; 2) is the encounter considered natural, supernatural, or borderline supernatural within the narrative of the saga; 3) is the proximity to the narrative middle consistent with the supernaturality of the encounter according to the hypothesis?

3.3 Definitions

3.3.1 Ófreskjur

Mundal states in her paper that "the sagas of Icelanders will normally underline the idea that the supernatural is something unusual more strongly than the fornaldarsögur,"[136] and uses the excellent example of the apparition of Gunnarr á Hlíðarenda in *Njáls saga* singing in his mound.[137] This event is thought to be so unbelievable that Njáll has to be told three times. This signifies how supernatural the event is perceived to be, as such things are not something that should happen on one's own doorstep. The inherent irony is that these things *never* happen anywhere else: draugar are always bound to the narrative middle,[138] especially inside farms as is also common in later Icelandic folklore, and encountering them is therefore less believable and more akin to the supernatural. In contrast, the protagonist may on the other hand wander upon a gargantuan beast in Austrvegr, let us suppose a flugdreki,[139] without feeling the least bit surprised; the flugdreki is simply part of the local fauna, no more out of the ordinary than regular beasts of burden, albeit considerably more violent, and thus the flugdreki is usually killed without much ado, let alone amazement.

---

[136]Mundal, Else 2006, 7

[137]See also Vésteinn Ólason. 2003, 158 and onwards.

[138]It has been pointed out to me that Grettis saga may be an exception from this as the hauntings take place in farms far away in secluded valleys. The argument is valid, but in this research I chose to not take geographical location of the farms into account and rather define the farms as designated narrative middles. I do not see this as a contradiction in terms as, however secluded the farms may be, which itself is a matter of debate, they are still the center of their inhabitants' everyday lives, and as such supernatural occurences would not be commonplace there. If they were they would not be considered supernatural, but ordinary, and ordinary events do not invoke wonder.

[139]A flying dragon.

In *Bjarnar saga Hítdœlakappa* it says:

> Um sumarit eptir fór Bjǫrn vestr til Englands ok fekk þar
> góða virðing ok var þar tvá vetr með Knúti inum ríka. Þar
> varð sá atburðr, er Bjǫrn fylgði konungi ok sigldi með liði
> sínu fyrir sunnan sjó,[140] at fló yfir lið konungs flugdreki
> ok lagðisk at þeim ok vildi hremma mann einn, en Bjǫrn
> var nær staddr ok brá skildi yfir hann, en hremmði hann
> næsta í gegnum skjǫldinn. Síðan grípr Bjǫrn í sporðinn
> drekans annarri hendi, en annarri hjó hann fyrir aptan
> vængina, ok gekk þar í sundr, ok fell drekinn niðr dauðr;
> en konungr gaf Birni mikit fé ok langskip gott, ok því helt
> hann til Danmerkr.[141]

In this scene, Bjǫrn Hítdœlakappi dispatches a flugdreki, while out
sailing, with hardly any effort. He easily grabs its tail with one hand
and cuts it in two with his sword in the other while saving his comrade.
Never in this narrative are any words used to describe wonder at the
flying dragon, nor is there any time used to dwell on the scene of this
amazing event or how the characters on board king Knútr's ship felt.

---

[140]Literally this means 'south of the sea'. This is a fixed phrase however, meaning
eather 'in Norway' or 'abroad'. I have chosen to use the wider meaning here, although
it is almost certain they were sailing somewhere in the Norwegian Ocean between
England and Denmark (Sigurður Nordal, Guðni Jónsson. 1938, 124.)

[141]Bjarnar saga Hítdœlakappa 1938, ch. 5. **Translation:** The next summer, Bjorn went
to England, and won much esteem there, and stayed for two years with King Canute
the Great. It happened, when Bjorn was accompanying the king, and sailing with his
company in southern seas, that a dragon flew over the king's company and attacked
them and tried to snatch one of the men. Bjorn then gripped the dragon's tail with one
hand, while with the other he struck behind the wings, and the dragon was severed,
and fell down dead. The king gave Bjorn a large sum of money and a fine longship;
with this he sailed to Denmark (The saga of Bjorn, champion of the Hitardal people
1997, 262.).

This is because the event is not at all considered to be amazing in any respect, that is why nothing is said of emotion. Bjǫrn is rewarded for his heroics, then the narrative ends with him sailing to Denmark. The event is never mentioned again. In *Brennu-Njáls saga*, Þorkell hákr kills both a flugdreki and a finngálkn:

> Þorkell hákr hafði farit utan ok framit sik í ǫðrom lǫndom. Hann hafði drepit spellvirkja austr á Jamtaskógi; síðan fór hann austr í Svíþjóð ok fór til lags með Sørkvi karli, ok herjuðu þaðan í Austrveg. En fyrir austan Bálagarðssíðu[142] átti Þorkell at sœkja þeim vatn eitt kveld; þá mœtti hann finngálkni ok varðisk því lengi, en svá lauk með þeim, at hann drap finngálknit. Þaðan fór hann austr í Aðalsýslu; þar vá hann at flugdreka.[143]

Again, we see that nothing seems to be out of the ordinary in this short narrative. Þorkell hákr kills wrongdoers in Jämtland, south of Lappland in modern day central Sweden. He then travels eastward, presumably to Lappland, and from there on to Austrvegr.[144] On his way there, he meets a finngálkn at Bálagarðssíða in Finland. They fight for a long while but in the end he kills the finngálkn. From there on he goes east to Aðalsýsla,[145] where he slays a flugdreki. The text is so nonchalant about this second killing that the reader can only assume that the dragon was attacking Þorkell, as nowhere does it say so. The description is furthermore so blatantly full of

---

[142]Most likely on the south-west coast of Finland (Einar Ól. Sveinsson. 1954, 302.)

[143]Brennu-Njáls saga 1954, ch. 119.

[144]Presumably the circum-Baltic countries, i.e. modern day southeast Finland, western Russia and the Baltic States.

[145]In the western part of modern day Estonia, Haapsalu. In ch. 30 of Njáls saga, Gunnarr, Kolskeggr and their men travel to Rafala (modern day Tallinn) and then to Eysýsla (modern day Saarema, off the coast of Haapsalu).

disinterest in these feats that one would think Þorkell hákr did this on a day to day basis. This indicates that these incidents are neither supernatural nor fantastic. On the contrary it seems quite normal to encounter flugdrekar and finngálkn around those parts. It is their natural habitat.

Daniel Sävborg has also noted this difference between the natural and the supernatural and takes two examples for his argument; it bears mentioning that his latter example is taken from a Fornaldarsaga, although it should not matter in this context.

The first incident Sävborg mentions is Hildiglúmr's vision in *Njáls saga*, where an apparition of a fiery rider approaches him with a prophecy that Njáll and his sons will soon be avenged. He proceeds in astonishment to tell his father, and then Hjalti Skeggjason, who tells him that he has witnessed a *gandreið*, and that such events are foreboding of ill tides. The second example is of Ketill hœngr's fight with a dragon:

> Eitt kveld eftir dagsetr tók Ketill öxi sína í hönd sér ok gekk norðr á eyna. En er hann var kominn eigi allskammt í burt frá bænum, sér hann dreka einn fljúga at sér norðan ór björgunum. Hann hafði lykkju ok sporð sem ormr, en vængi sem dreki. Eldr þótti honum brenna ór augum hans ok gini. Eigi þóttist Ketill slíkan fisk sét hafa eða nokkura óvætti aðra, því at hann vildi heldr eiga at verjast fjölda manna. Dreki sjá sótti at honum, en Ketill varðist með öxinni vel ok karlmannliga. Svá gekk lengi, allt þar til at Ketill gat höggvit á lykkjuna ok þar í sundr drekann. Datt hann þá niðr dauðr.[146]

---

[146]Ketils saga hœngs 1954, Ch. 1. **My translation:** One evening after nightfall, Ketill

Again we see the same thing as before. Sävborg argues that: "I berättelsen om Hildiglúmr och hans möte med häxryttaren skildras det övernaturliga som något som egentligen hör till en annan värld", but in the case of Ketill hængr "finns ingen knall och inget skalv eller något annat som antyder att en gräns till en annan värld överträds. Der finns ingen antydan om att draken skulle höra hemma i en annan värld än vi."[147] He goes on to say that "Mötena med de övernaturliga varelserna framställs som självklara fakta av samma slag som övriga äventyr".[148] The reason for this is that these creatures are in fact not in any way supernatural.

A counter-argument might of course be that the world of the Fornaldarsögur is more 'fantastic' or otherwise unbelievable than the world of the Íslendingasögur, like Mundal and others have argued, and it is because of this that the dreki in Ketils saga hœngs does not seem to be supernatural. Such an argument would fail to recognize that the drekar of the Íslendingasögur behave more or less in exactly the same way and serve the same literary purpose: to prove a character's valour in combat. There is no indication that such creatures are any more out of the ordinary in the realistic sagas. Daniel Sävborg also mentions Max Lüthi's definition of 'Sagen und Märchen' and dismisses it in the case of Íslendingasögur on the same grounds as

---

picked up his axe and walked to the northern side of the island. But when he had walked a good deal away from the house he saw a dragon flying towards him north from the cliffside. It had coils and a tail like a worm, but wings like a dragon. It seemed to him that fire burnt in its eyes and mouth. Ketill did not think he had ever seen such a fish or any other such foul beings, and that he would rather defend himself from many men. This dragon attacked him, but Ketill defended himself well and in a manly manner with his axe. This went on for a long time, until Ketill was able to give a blow to the coils and cut the dragon in half. Then it fell down dead.

[147]Sävborg, Daniel. 2009, 324.
[148]Sävborg, Daniel. 2009, 335.

I do when it comes to the distinction between the supernatural and
the fantastic – that it simply does not apply to the material at hand:
"Den norröna litteraturen har sina egna unika genrer och genrelagar;
en islänningasaga är förvisso ingen sägen och fornaldarsagan ingen
folksaga".[149]

3.3.2 Tröll

The word tröll can mean many separate things, to quote Ármann
Jakobsson:

1. Tröll getur verið samheiti við „jötunn" eða „bergbúi", tiltölulega
   lítt skilgreind annarsheimsvættur í óbyggðum, með yfirbragði
   manns en stundum ansi stórvaxin eða ljót.

2. Oft er tröll lýsandi orð, notað til að lýsa miklu afli, styrk og
   stærð.

3. Orðið tröll er mjög oft notað til að lýsa fjölkynngi [. . .]

4. Ef til vill þess vegna geta ekki aðeins risar eða jötnar verið tröll
   heldur einnig illir andar eða draugar, eins og Sóti og Ögmundur
   Eyþjófsbani.

5. Orðið tröll er stundum notað um hamskipti og berserkur getur
   verið tröll. Sögnin trylla virðist einnig stundum vísa til ham-
   skipta en sögnin hamast er líka notuð.

---

[149]Sävborg, Daniel. 2009, 326.

6. Notkun orðsins er almennt fremur neikvæð. Stundum er orðið notað nánast sem uppnefni eða blótsyrði og þá er kannski ýmsu vísað í trölla hendur.

7. Langalgengast er að menn kalli andstæðinga sína tröll en fá dæmi um að neinn noti orðið um sjálfan sig og síst af öllu gera mennskir menn það.

8. Tröll eru framandi.

9. Orðið vísar gjarnan til ákveðinna eiginleika. Tröll geta verið ónæm fyrir járni. Tröll bíta menn á barkann (eins og Egill Skalla-Grímsson gerir raunar einnig enda er honum eitt sinn líkt við tröll). Tröll eru líka stundum mannætur. Í stuttu máli: tröllskapurinn virðist tengjast eiginleikum og hegðun.

10. Í Grettis sögu kemur fram sú skoðun að tröll heyri ekki til dags-birtunni og þarf ekki að koma á óvart í ljósi nýlegri þjóðsagna.[150]

11. Vígfúsir blámenn geta verið tröll.

12. Brunnmigar eru tröll.

13. Dýr geta verið tröll, að minnsta kosti þau sem mögnuð eru upp af fjölkunnugum manni.

14. Heiðnar vættir eru tröll.

15. Ef til vill merkir orðið bæði þann sem vekur upp óvætti með göldrum og óvættina sjálfa.

---

[150] Ármann refers here to tenths of Icelandic folktales on tröll who turn to stone in the sunlight. Cf. Jón Árnason. 2003, which I have referred to before in this thesis.

16. Ekki aðeins getur draugur verið tröll heldur einnig dýr andsetið
af honum og má þá velta því fyrir sér hvort tröllið er þá dýrið
sjálft eða andinn sem hefur tekið það yfir.

17. Tröll eru ásamt djöflum, seiðskröttum og heiðingjum helstu and-
stæðingar kristni og réttrar trúar.[151]

---

[151]Ármann Jakobsson. 2008a, 105-110. **My translation:** 1) Tröll can be synonymous
with "jötunn" or "bergbúi", a relatively poorly defined otherworld-being in the wilder-
ness, with the appearance of a man but sometimes enormous in size or ugly. 2) Often,
tröll is a descriptive term, used to denote great power, strength and size. 3) The word
tröll is very often used to describe fjölkynngi [the ability to perform magic]. 4) Perhaps
for that reason not only risar or jötnar can be tröll, but also evil spirits or draugar,
like Sóti and Ögmundur Eyþjófsbani. 5) The word tröll is sometimes used to describe
shapeshifting and a berserker can be a tröll. The verb trylla sometimes seems to refer
to shapeshifting but the verb hamast is also used. 6) The usage of the word is generally
rather negative. Sometimes it is used almost as a bad name or a curse word, and some
things may at some points be wished into the hands of tröll. 7) Most commonly people
call their adversaries tröll, but few examples are of people using it to refer to themselves,
and least of all do humans do so. 8) Tröll are exotic. 9) The word most often refers to
certain properties. Tröll can be impervious to iron. Tröll bite peoples' throats (like Egill
Skalla-Grímsson in fact also does and he is at one point likened to a tröll). Sometimes
tröll are also cannibals. In short: the trolldom seems to be connected to characteristics
and behaviour. 10) In Grettis saga, the opinion is voiced that tröll do not belong to
the daylight, which does not have to come to anyone's surprise in light of more recent
folktales. 11) Blámenn warriors can be tröll. 12) Brunnmigar [those who urinate in the
water supply] are tröll. 13) Animals can be tröll, at least those that are conjured by a
man who is fjölkunnugur (sorcerer). 14) Pagan beings are tröll. 15) Perhaps the word
means both the one who conjures up evil beings and the evil beings themselves. 16)
Not only can a draugur be a tröll, but also an anmial possessed by a draugur, which
gives reason to speculate whether the tröll is the animal itself or the spirit that possesses
it. 17) Tröll are, along with devils, sorcerers and pagans, the greatest adversaries of
Christianity and the right faith.

Tröll are of a more ambiguous nature than ófreskjur and draugar and therefore they have been placed between them on the x axis relating to geographical distance and on the y axis relating to the supernatural, as they neither pertain to one more than the other. As has been extensively argued by Ármann Jakobsson, the various types of tröll are ambiguous creatures of habitat and character, and by all reasoning may be considered half-human as they both are the ancestors of humankind and share with them a certain bond.[152] Ármann points out that in *Hrólfs saga Gautrekssonar*, it is behaviour that defines a tröll "rather than anything else", and that when Þórir járnskjöldr appears in the hallway of the king's castle he is perceived to be a tröll: var tröll svá mikit komit í hallardyrin, at enginn þóttist séð hafa jafnmikit tröll [. . .] Þetta tröll var svá grimt ok ógrligt, at engi þorði til útgöngu at leita":[153] Until identified "A non-threatening and familiar being cannot be a 'tröll'. Once the being has been recognized it ceases to frighten and loses some of its trollish aspects".[154]

Tröll do not live among humans but tend to live in the mountains, on a liminal plane, much like the trolls of Icelandic folklore.[155] Of a similar nature are the blámenn, who are neither considered human nor beast, and sometimes they are also reputed to be 'tröll'.[156] Tröll invoke fear and they sometimes intrude on human grounds, though

---

[152]Ármann Jakobsson. 2006, Ármann Jakobsson. 2009b,

[153]Ármann Jakobsson. 2009b, 192. **His translation:** "such a great troll was in the doors of the cstle that none claimed to have seen such a big troll [. . .] this troll was so cruel and terrifying that nobody dared to venture out, such was the terror that went with this beast".

[154]Ármann Jakobsson. 2009b, 192-193.

[155]Cf. Kumlbúa þáttr 1986, Bárðar saga Snæfellsáss 1986, and the abundant number of folktales about trolls in the collection of Íslenskar þjóðsögur og ævintýri (Jón Árnason. 2003)

[156]Kjalnesinga saga 1986, ch. 15

many times it is the other way around. Battles with tröll are usually more extensively described than battles with finngálkn or drekar. This I would argue is because tröll are less common[157] and more out of the ordinary, and their significantly more evil nature garners that much more attention.[158] If tröll are not considered 'ordinary' yet still are well known in the saga universe, they must be considered borderline supernatural. Most of them also share more characteristics with humans than with animals, so they are harder to identify and are therefore more dangerous, all the while living closer to the habitat of humans which makes them even more of a threat.

Ármann Jakobsson supposes that tröll can possibly be considered to be the opposite of correct knowledge, to the right faith, to society and to God's law. Their main purpose would then be to represent the inverse of what is right and to be enemies of society. The same can also be said of magic and its practicioners, which may explain why magic and tröll cannot be easily separated. Whichever form the tröll takes, blámaður, draugur or else, its intrinsic nature is that of the magical and the negative, which also explains the word's negative connotations. Moreover it is not clear whether medieval Icelanders would have agreed on a definition of what a tröll is. Ármann's conclusion is that tröll is all wisdow that is not positive, true and given by God, everything which is unfamiliar, exotic and inhuman.[159] Given their ambiguous nature, tröll would certainly have been thought of as *mirabilia* bordering on *miracula* in the Middle Ages, and in that regard their placing on the boundary of society, as shown in the figure of the narrative model, seems fitting.

---

[157]They are, in fact, far more common in Íslendingasögur than battles with drekar or finngálkn, but in the saga world they are not considered to be common.

[158]Cf. Orms þáttr Stórólfssonar 1986, Ketils saga hœngs 1954.

[159]Ármann Jakobsson. 2008a, 110-111.

3.3.3 Draugar

Conversely, draugar would have been thought of as mirabilia bordering on magica in the Middle Ages. Draugar have a different relation to the narrative middle than the previous two groups of beings. In most cases the protagonist must travel to encounter tröll, and in all cases he must do so to encounter ófreskjur. The protagonist could never expect to encounter draugar during these travels as they would be waiting for him at home, stoking the fire if you will, which incidentally is where he never would expect to encounter them. Draugar and afturgöngur are deceased people who have returned from their graves and they seldom travel far from home. For this reason they will most often haunt their old farmstead were they used to live, although sometimes they seem to be capable of roaming around its general vicinity or around the settled region of the countryside; their powers do not seem to transcend the outskirts of settled areas. Their motive is usually malevolent and personal.

When a person comes back from the dead a natural law is broken, "det finns en gräns mellan vår värld och den övernaturliga och [...] möten med de övernaturliga är i grunden onormala och sällsynta".[160] It is this characteristic that truly differentiates draugar and afturgöngur from the two other groups and what characterizes their supernaturality in the eye of the beholder, i.e. the ability or affinity to strike where we would least suspect it and where we are at our most vulnerable: at home. As Sävborg has observed, quoting Lüthi:

Max Lüthi påpekar i sina undersökningar att de över-

---

[160]Sävborg, Daniel. 2009, 332.

naturliga varelserna i sägnerna befinner sig nära män-
niskornas hemmiljö. Tros att berättelserna framhäver att
de tillhör en annan värld är de "dem Menschen äußerlich
nahe. Sie wohnen in seinem Hause, in seinem Acker, im
nahen Wald oder Fluß, Berg oder See" [...] I folksagan
är det tvärtom. Trots att dess övernaturliga varelser inte
tycks tillhöra en annan värld än människorna håller de
till färran från människorna: "Selten trifft der Held sie
in seinem Hause oder in seinem Dorf; er begegnet ih-
nen, wenn er in die Ferne wandert" [...] Detta förhållande
påminner om vad vi fann i de "klassiska" islännngasagorna:
det finns ett samband mellan den isländska spelplatsen
– sagahjältarnas hemmiljö – och distansmarkörer liksom
ett samband mellan frånvaron av distansmarkörer och en
spelplats i främmande länder.[161]

The undead are creatures that have lost their humanity, they are no
longer the person their embodiment should represent. In fact the
bodies themselves seem to have few or any human qualities. This is
shown the description of Þórólfr bægifótur's dead body in *Eyrbyggja
saga*: "Var hann þá enn ófúinn ok inn trollsligsti at sjá. Hann var blár
sem hel ok digr sem naut."[162] He looks like a 'tröll', not a man. His
subsequent afturganga, added with his ability to possess livestock,
gives rise to the reasoning that in death he has more in common with
a demon than the person he used to be,[163] even though he was a foul

---

[161]Sävborg, Daniel. 2009, 345. quoting Lüthi 1992, 10-11.

[162]Eyrbyggja saga 1935, ch. 63 **Translation:** still unrotted and monstrous to look at.
He was black as Hell and as huge as an ox. The saga of the people of Eyri 1997, 212.
The word 'hel' in this context more likely refers to death than to Hell.

[163]On the ambiguity of differentiating between ghosts and demons, see Ármann
Jakobsson. 2010.

person while still alive. That which takes human form yet is not human is by all reasoning the most supernatural of all dangerous beings, and also the most powerful and dangerous one.[164] Their reluctance to leave the house makes hauntings that much more serious.

In spite of this, afturgöngur were not in every respect unexpected, as sometimes precautions were made to prevent the deceased from returning from the dead. This is done with the body of Þórólfr bægifótur. His son Arnkell takes every precaution not to disturb his father's still sitting corpse and prepares it in such a manner that it should not be able to come back from the dead, even covering its eyes so that none may be harmed by its gaze,[165] as is reported to have happened in other sagas, most notably in *Grettis saga* when Grettir battles with Glámr's afturganga. Here are the measures Arnkell takes according to *Eyrbyggja saga*:

> Gekk Arnkell nú inn í eldaskálann ok svá inn eptir setinu á bak Þórólfi; hann bað hvern at varask at ganga framan at honum, meðan honum váru eigi nábjargir veittar; tók Arnkell þá í herðar Þórólfi, ok varð hann at kenna aflsmunar, áðr hann kœmi honum undir; síðan sveipaði hann klæðum at hǫfði Þórólfi ok bjó um hann eptir siðvenju. Eptir þat lét hann brjóta vegginn á bak honum ok draga hann þar út. Síðan váru yxn fyrir sleða beittir; var Þórólfr þar í lagiðr, ok óku honum upp í Þórsárdal, ok var þat eigi þrautarlaust, áðr hann kom í þann stað, sem hann skyldi vera; dysjuðu þeir Þórólf þar rammliga.[166]

---

[164] Ármann Jakobsson. 2010, 192 noted that "Óvættur er þeim mun magnaðri eftir því sem erfiðara verður að flokka hana, skilgreina eða gefa nafn."

[165] Ármann Jakobsson. 2010, 204.

[166] Eyrbyggja saga 1935, ch. 33 **Translation:** Then Arnkel went into the fire-room, and

But all his precautions are to no avail. Þórólfr returns soon after so that no one is safe after nightfall. The cattle used to drag his body become 'trollriða', possessed, and all livestock venturing too close to his mound become irrevocably disturbed. Soon after that people start dying, and for a reason never given they are all buried alongside Þórólfr only to be later seen in his macabre company.[167] This goes on until every farm in the region has been abandoned, after which his body is moved to another location.

Þórólfr then returns after Arnkell's death and resumes his posthumous misanthropy. Finally his body is burned, yet with much trouble, for the fire does not seem to affect him at all at first. When he is at last burned his ashes get caught in the wind and blown out to the shoreline where a cow licks it off the rocks. The cow later gives birth to the calf Glæsir, which is possessed by Þórólfr and later kills its owner Þóroddr.[168]

Similar measures are taken when Skalla-Grímr Kveld-Úlfsson passes away on his bed:

> Skalla-grímr kom heim um miðnættisskeið ok gekk þá
> til rúms síns ok lagðisk niðr í klæðum sínum; en um
> morgininn, er lýsti ok menn klæddusk, þá sat Skalla-Grímr

walked up along the benches behind Thorolf. He told everytone to beware of walking in front of him until his eyes had been closed. Then Arnkel took hold of Thorolf's shoulders and he had to exert more force than he expected in order to move him. He wrapped some clothes around Thorolf's head and prepared his body according to the customs of the time. After that he had the wall behind him broken down to drag the body outside. Oxen were harnessed to a sled on which Thorolf's corpse was laid, which was then driven up into Thorsardal, but not withouth a lot of effort, until he was brought to the place where he was to be buried. They buried Thorolf in a strongly-built cairn. The saga of the people of Eyri 1997, 173.

[167] Eyrbyggja saga 1935, ch. 34

[168] Eyrbyggja saga 1935, ch. 63

fram á stokk ok var þá andaðr ok svá stirðr, at menn fengu hvergi rétt hann né hafit, ok var alls við leitat. Þá var hesti skotit undir einn mann; hleypði sá sem ákafligast, til þess er hann kom á Lambastaði; gekk hann þegar á fund Egils ok segir honum þessi tíðendi. Þá tók Egill vápn sín ok klæði ok reið heim til Borgar um kveldit, ok þegar hann hafði af baki stigit, gekk hann inn ok í skot, er var um eldahúsit, en dyrr váru fram ór skotinu at setum innan-verðum. Gekk Egill fram í setit ok tók í herðar Skalla-Grími ok kneikði hann aptr á bak, lagði hann niðr í setit ok veitti honum þá nábjargir; þá bað Egill taka graftól ok br-jóta vegginn fyrir sunnan. Ok er þat var gǫrt, þá tók Egill undir hǫfðahlut Skalla-Grími, en aðrir tóku fótahlutinn; báru þeir hann um þvert húsit ok svá út í gegnum veg-ginn, þar er áðr var brotinn. Báru þeir hann þá í hríðinni ofan í Naustanes; var þar tjaldat yfir um nóttina; en um morgininn at flóði var lagðr Skalla-Grímr í skip ok róit með hann út til Digraness. Lét Egill þar gera haug á framan-verðu nesinu; var þar í lagðr Skalla-Grímr ok hestr hans ok vápn hans ok smíðartól; ekki er þess getit, at lausafé væri lagt í haug hjá honum.[169]

---

[169]Egils saga Skalla-Grímssonar 1933, ch. 58 **Translation:** Skallagrim came home in the middle of the night, went to his bed and lay down, still wearing his clothes. At daybreak next morning, when everybody was getting dressed, Skallagrim was sitting on the edge of his bed, dead, and so stiff that they could neither straighten him out nor lift him no matter how they tried. A horse was saddled quickly and the rider set off at full pelt all the way to Lambastadir. He went straight to see Egil and told him the news. Egil took his weapons and clothes and rode back to Borg that evening. He dismounted, entered the house and went to an alcove in the fire-room where there was a door through to the benches where people slept and sat. Egil went through to the bench, took Skallagrim by the shoulders and tugged him backwards. He laid him

The immediacy of these actions is the first thing that the reader notices. Immediately when Skalla-Grímr's body has been discovered a rider is dispatched to Lambastaðir to notify Egill, who quickly gets himself ready and rides out homeward. Like Arnkell, Egill does not confront his father from the front, but goes by an elaborate path to come at him from behind. They both make sure that nobody catches the dead man's gaze, and immediately after the posthumous arrangements have been made they head out with the corpse to bury it. The trip takes two days and it is specifically said that they made no rest until they made camp in Naustanes. They then have to sail by boat to Digranes where he finally is buried. Customary burial items follow Skalla-Grímr into his grave, including his horse which apparently someone rode alongside the troop of pallbearers. While the others rowed from Naustanes a long way out of the fjord, round a peninsula into the bay next to it, the rider must then have crossed country. This seems like an awful lot of work by modern standards just to earth a corpse, but in this case due to all these precautions, Egill and his men are saved from the trouble of having to deal with Skalla-Grímr's afturganga. Although it seems that Egill and Arnkell dealt with their fathers' dead bodies in exactly the same way, it only prevented one of them from returning from his grave.

In Gísla saga, Þorgrímr Þorsteinsson offers to tie Vésteinn's body

down on the bench and closed his nostrils, eyes and mouth. Then he ordered the men to take spades and break down the south wall. When this had been done, Egil took hold of him by the head and shoulders, and the others by his legs. They carried him like this right across the house and out through where the wall had been broken down. Then they carried him right out to Naustanes and covered his body up for the night. In the morning, at high tide, Skallagrim's body was put in a ship and they rowed with it out to Digranes. Egil had a mound made on the edge of the promontory, where Skallagrim was laid to rest with his horse and weapons and tools It is not mentioned whether any money was put into his tomb. Egil's saga 1997, 115

helskór (death shoes) with which he could walk to Valhöll, adding that it is customary. This is a strange statement as it should be expected that Vésteinn's mourners already know what is customary and what is not, which gives Gísli a reason to believe that it was Þorgrímr who murdered Vésteinn and is trying to hide it with a kind gesture. Gísli proceeds to avenge Vésteinn by killing Þorgrímr in his bed. When he receives word of Þorgrímr's murder he offers to pay for his funeral:

> „Skammt er þá milli illra verka og stórra," segir Gísli; „Viljum vér til þess bjóðast að heygja Þorgrím og eigið þér það að oss er það skylt að vér gerum það með sæmd." Þetta þiggja þeir og fara allir saman á Sæból til haugsgerðar og leggja Þorgrím í skip. Nú verpa þeir hauginn eftir fornum sið. Og er búið er að lykja hauginn þá gengur Gísli til óssins og tekur upp stein einn, svo mikinn sem bjarg væri, og leggur í skipið svo að nær þótti hvert tré hrökkva fyrir en brakaði mjög í skipinu og mælti: „Eigi kann eg skip að festa ef þetta tekur veður upp." Það var nokkurra manna mál að eigi þótti allólíkt fara því er Þorgrímur hafði gert við Véstein er hann ræddi um helskóna.[170]

---

[170]Gísla saga Súrssonar 1943, ch. 17 **Translation:** "Great deeds and ill deeds often fall within each other's shadow," said Gisli. "We will take it upon ourselves to make a burial mound for Thorgrim. This we owe you, and it is our duty to carry it out with honour." They accepted his offer and all returned to Saebol together to build a mound. They laid Thorgrim out in a boat and raised the mound in accordance with the old ways. When the mound had been sealed, Gisli walked to the mouth of the river and lifted a stone so heavy it was more like a boulder. He dropped it into the boat with such a resounding crash that almost every plank of wood gave way. "If the weather shifts this," he said, "then I don't know how to fasten a boat." Some people remakred that this was not unlike what Thorgrim had done with Vestein when he spoke of the Hel-shoes. Gisli Sursson's saga 1997, 20

Gísli mimics Þorgrímr from Vésteinn's funeral with a custom that is perceived to be strange; no doubt in both cases to prevent their victims from returning from death to reveal the truth or harm them in any other way. Neither of them comes back, yet Þorgrímr and Gísli's blatant acts of overdoing it at their victims' funerals reveal their crime and as a result they both succumb to their fate. So in a sense there is no direct need for the involvement of afturgöngur.

Even though the walking dead are in some ways an expected possibility, they nonetheless always strike with terror into the hearts of men and cause them to feel disbelief at what is happening, as if no one could have predicted that the dead would actually rise from their graves in reality. This indicates that the burial rites were customary out of superstition and not as a precaution; so it seems such rites did not have any practical foundation at all, but that they were rather just the way it was done. Draugar and afturgöngur belonged to the realm of the supernatural, they were a phenomenon that people spoke of as real, yet they could not exist without first breaking the laws of God and reason. In that sense they were an impossibility, and therefore I claim here that encounters with draugar and afturgöngur are the only ones in Íslendingasögur that are absolutely and in all ways supernatural. They are *mirabilia* bordering on *magica*.

3.4 Encounters with uncanny beings in Íslendingasögur

Now we come to the analysis ef encounters with uncanny beings in Íslendingasögur, based on the criteria and definitions presented above.

3.4.1 Ófreskjur

Most of the examples of ófreskjur in Íslendingasögur have already
been mentioned. In *Njáls saga*, Þorkell hákr slays a finngálkn east of
Bálagarðssíða (Finland) and a flugdreki in Aðalsýsla (Estonia). Both
countries are on the narrative periphery of the saga universe. Both the
finngálkn and the flugdreki are easily dealt with and do not matter
within the larger scope of the saga. These encounters do not invoke
any sense of disbelief within the narrative and are not considered to
be out of the ordinary; on the contrary the encounters seem natural
and the creatures seem to belong within the accepted reality of *Njáls
saga*.

In *Bjarnar saga Hítdœlakappa* a flugdreki appears and attacks king
Knútr's ship. After having saved his comrade from the flugdreki,
Bjǫrn grabs its tail and with ease he swiftly cuts it in half with his
sword. This event takes place either on the coastline of Norway, in
the Norwegian ocean between England and Denmark, or abroad in
an unspecified location, so it is unclear whether the encounter takes
place in a liminal space or on the narrative periphery. As with Þorkell
hákr's narrative, this encounter with a flugdreki does not invoke any
sense of disbelief within the narrative and the creature seems to be an
accepted part of the reality of *Bjarnar saga Hítdœlakappa*.

Þórir in *Þorskfirðinga saga* (also called *Gull-Þóris saga*) travels with
his friends northwards through Finnmörk until they reach Dumbshaf.[171] There they enter a cave behind a waterfall where dragons lie
sleeping on top of piles of gold. They attack the dragons, killing some
of them, but the dragons retaliate. One of them grabs his comrade
Þrándr in its mouth and they all fly out of the cave. Outside, Bjǫrn no-

---

[171]The North Sea.

tices that the greatest dragon has a man in its mouth and jabs it with a spear. Poisoned blood spews over Bjǫrn's face from the wound, killing him quickly, while Hyrningr gets some on his foot, crippling him. Meanwhile, Þórir and the others in the cave load up on gold before returning to the others. Þórir strokes Hyrningr's foot, healing him.

This encounter takes place beyond the narrative periphery of the saga, in a cave in one of the most remote possible places. Yet these drekar are more powerful than drekar from other Íslendingasögur, and unlike in the other narratives we get to know that they hoard gold. When they encounter the drekar, it is simply stated that "þeir heyrðu blástur til drekanna", they heard the dragons blowing. Previously in the saga they hear the story of the viking Valr and his sons who carried their gold into this cavern, lay upon it and turned into drekar, and for this reason they seek out the cavern. So these are not in any sense ordinary drekar, yet they do not invoke a sense of disbelief. *Þorskfirðinga saga* seems to adhere to an altogether different principle of what is possible and what is impossible than the other Íslendingasögur containing drekar, but by the standards of other sagas these drekar would not be considered supernatural either, but borderline supernatural in the same way tröll are.

In the end, Þórir himself turns into a dreki:

> Þat var sagt, eitthvert sumar at Guðmundr, sonr hans, hafði fallit í bardaga, en þat hafði þó logit verit. Þóri brá svá við þessi tíðendi, er hann frétti, at hann hvarf á brott frá búi sínu, ok vissi engi maðr, hvat af honum væri orðit eða hann kom niðr, en þat hafa menn fyrir satt, at hann hafi at dreka orðit ok hafi lagizt á gullkistur sínar. Helzt þat ok lengi síðan, at menn sá dreka fljúga ofan um þeim megin

frá Þórisstöðum, ok Gullfors er kallaðr, ok yfir fjörðinn í
fjall þat, er stendr yfir bænum í Hlíð.[172]

This story is especially interesting for two reasons: it is *believed* that
Þórir turned into a dragon, although the wording indicates that this is
uncertain, and it is the only saga where a dreki is seen in Iceland, even
though these sightings seem to be unverified as previously said. This
dreki is also different from most other drekar in the Íslendingasögur
in the way that it is the mythical sort of dreki; a human being, Þórir,
turns into a dreki, lives in the mountains and sometimes can be seen
flying around. The dreki however never penetrates the boundary
between the mythical world and the human world, and the story of
its true identity seems to me to serve the purpose of striking awe in the
minds of those who hear it. It is in fact something that people normally
would not believe in, hence the assuring words "það hafa menn fyrir
satt" which would translate to either 'it is generally acknowledged'
or 'people regard this as fact'. The dreki Þórir is thus different in
character by consequence of geography. If his habitat was in Sweden,
Finland or Estonia it would not be as important in respect to the
narrative, and therefore he is more supernatural than the other drekar,
all the while still respecting the boundary between the two worlds and
living on some sort of liminal plane which seems impossible to access.

---

[172]Þorskfirðinga saga 1986, ch. 20. **Translation:** One summer it was reported that his
son Gudmund had died in a battle, but this was only a lie. Thorir was so startled when
he heard the news that he disappeared from his farm. No one knew what happened
to him or where he ended up, but people believe that he turned into a dragon, and
lay down on his gold chests. It also happened for a long time afterwards that people
saw a dragon flying down from the mountains above Thorisstadir – at the place called
Gullfoss (Gold Falls) – and over the fjord to the mountain that rises above the farm at
Hlid. (Gold-Thorir's saga 1997, 359.)

Finally, *Finnboga saga ramma* presents us with an interesting scenario in which Gunnbjǫrn must fight the viking Rauðr. At first it may seem that Rauðr has an "excellent dragon" fighting on his side, then when Gunnbjǫrn vanquishes Rauðr the dragon is his yet is never again mentioned in the saga. This would be an interesting plot twist indeed, but in this instance the word *dreki* most certainly refers to a kind of longship.

The result of this analysis can be viewed in the table in *figure 9*. It is structured to show the perfect result, e.g. a creature which according to the hypothesis should belong to the narrative periphery should also belong to the saga universe and therefore be considered natural. The individual sagas are listed vertically on the left hand side of the table and the result of the analysis is on the right hand side. The dark-coloured fields indicate where the perfect hypothesised result was not reached.

The drekar in the cave in *Þorskfirðingasaga* are found beyond the narrative periphery and belong naturally to the saga universe, yet they used to be human as per the ambiguity of tröll, which does not fit the criteria. Thus they only meet one of the two necessary conditions: their placing on the world map. That said, humans turning into drekar is a common medieval motif, but it is uncertain whether this applies to all drekar. These drekar could as a consequence just as well fit in the same category as tröll, as *mirabilia* bordering on *miracula*, an ambiguously human/animal sort of natural creature.

Þórir turns into a dreki and appears to live outside of reachable geography on a liminal plane, much like Bárðr Snæfellsás, whose nature is never certain, turns into a tröll and leaves society for the mountains. He thus fits more in with the tröll than with the ófreskjur and in that respect he deviates from the category of ófreskjur.

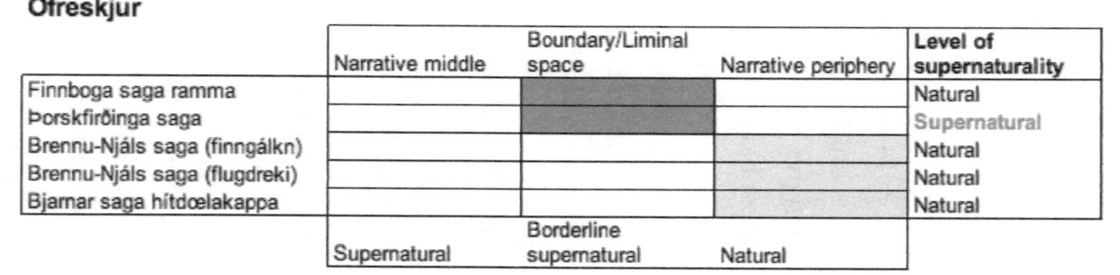

Ófreskjur

	Narrative middle	Boundary/Liminal space	Narrative periphery	Level of supernaturality
Finnboga saga ramma				Natural
Þorskfirðinga saga				Supernatural
Brennu-Njáls saga (finngálkn)				Natural
Brennu-Njáls saga (flugdreki)				Natural
Bjarnar saga hítdœlakappa				Natural
	Supernatural	Borderline supernatural	Natural	

Figure 9: Ófreskjur in Íslendingasögur

The flugdreki in *Bjarnar saga hítdœlakappa* strikes out at sea. It is not clear whether this happens close to shore or not, although this must be considered very likely as navigational technology is now not considered to have been as advanced as previously thought; while latitude was easily calculable, longitude was not.[173] Sailing by the shoreline would therefore have been the desired choice whenever it was possible. Drekar also seem to be exclusively land-based animals according to the sagas, so it is unlikely that Bjǫrn and his comrades were sailing out at sea although I will not exclude the possibility. It follows that this narrative most likely took place close to the coastline somewhere abroad as per the wider meaning of the fixed phrase 'fyrir sunnan sjó', and therefore it takes place either on the narrative periphery of the saga or in a liminal space, although I consider the latter possibility less likely. Both possibilities have been marked in the table. This encounter seems to be in concordance with the acceptable reality of the saga world, and thus the flugdreki does not break the laws of nature.

In further support of the hypothesis, the finngálkn and the flug-dreki Þorkell hákr battles with in *Brennu-Njáls saga* seem to be natural in all respects. Þorkell fights the finngálkn east of Bálagarðssíða in western Finland, on the narrative periphery, and the flugdreki he consequently fights is close to Haapsalu in Estonia, also on the narrative periphery. Neither battle is presented as an unbelievable tall-tale and these ófreskjur do not break the laws of nature.

Three out of the five encounters analysed here are in support of the hypothesis, whereas the fourth as it turns out belongs rather in the category with tröll, and considering the connection between magic and tröll it thereby is in some respects also consistent with the

---

[173]Cf. Þorsteinn Vilhjálmsson. 2001, 107-120. Sverrir Jakobsson. 2010, 233-236.

hypothesis.

3.4.2 Tröll

Encounters with tröll in Íslendingasögur are far more common than encounters with ófreskjur and by the same token it is easier to produce more tangible results. As I have previously mentioned I have excluded all acts of galdr, seiðr and fjölkynngi from this analysis for the sake of brevity (though it is prudent to mention that a preliminary study of mine, including accounts of sorcery, indicates not much deviation from the hypothesized model). Ármann Jakobsson has in the last 14 years published more research on tröll than anyone else and so my analysis presented in *figure 10* is mostly based on his work.

Bárðar saga Snæfellsáss is by far the most complicated example of tröll in Íslendingasögur and for this reason I find it fitting to start my analysis there. From the onset it is clear that Bárðr is not of regular lineage, as his father is a descendant of risar on his father's side but tröll on his mother's side:

> Hann var kominn af risakyni í föðurætt sína, ok er þat vænna fólk ok stærra en aðrir menn, en móðir hans var komin af tröllaættum, ok brá því Dumbi í hvárutveggja ætt sína, því at hann var bæði sterkr ok vænn ok góðr viðskiptis, ok kunni því at eiga allt sambland við mennska menn. En um þat brá honum í sitt móðurkyn, at hann var bæði sterkr ok stórvirkr ok umskiptasamr ok illskiptinn, ef honum eigi líkaði nökkut; vildi hann einn ráða við þá, er norðr þar váru, enda gáfu þeir honum konungs nafn, því at þeim þótti mikil forstoð í honum vera fyrir risum ok tröllum ok óvættum; var ok hann inn mesti bjargvættr

öllum þeim, er til hans kölluðu.[174]

Here there is a distinction made between tröll and risar, which is
unique in Íslendingasögur. These races seem to be at the "opposite
ends of the binary divide of good and evil" as Ármann Jakobsson
puts it, yet risar "are, in fact, referred to as 'menn' (humans) in the
saga, and their interracial marriage seems not in any sense to be out
of the ordinary."[175] Dumbr in fact is king of Dumbshaf, where Þórir
encounters the dragons in Þorskfirðinga saga, and so it appears that it
is normal to have a semi-supernatural king in this country. His son
Bárðr moves to Iceland after Dumbr is killed in battle with the þurs
Harðverkr, thus shifting the narrative middle out to the Atlantic while
bringing his semi-supernatural traits he inherited with him; from the
perspective of Icelanders he belongs to the periphery of the world as
the drekar in Dumbshaf did in Þorskfirðinga saga.

The final confrontation in Bárðar saga is particularly interesting for
the fact that in this narrative Gestr first calls upon his father Bárðr to
come to his aid, but when he arrives "orkaði Bárðr öngu. Færðu þeir
hinir dauðu hann í reikuð svo hann náði hvergi í nánd að koma."[176]
Bárðr shares with Óláfr the ability to appear when summoned, yet

---

[174]Bárðar saga Snæfellsáss 1986, ch. 1. **Translation:** He was descended from giants
on his father's side, a good-looking people and larger than other men; but his mother
was descended from the tribe of trolls. This double descent was evident in Dumb for
he was strapping and handsome, as well as good-tempered, so that he was readily able
to mingle with human beings. He took after his mother's side for he was not only
sturdy and ready for great deeds, but also shifty and vicious if something was not to
his liking. He wanted to become the sole ruler of the North, and they gave him the
name of king because it seemed to them that he would be a great defence against giants,
trolls, and evil beings. He was also the greatest guardian of all those who called upon
him. (Bard's saga 1997, 237.)

[175]Ármann Jakobsson. 2006, 1.

[176]Bárðar saga Snæfellsáss 1986, ch. 20.

Bárðr is mortal and Óláfr is a saint. Bárðr however is not powerful enough to help Gestr and it is after Bárðr's unsuccessful intervention that Gestr cries out to Óláfr helgi, who helps him win the battle, and subsequently reverts to Christianity for which his father Bárðr issues capital punishment. Ármann Jakobsson noted that: "After he has agreed to be baptised, his father Bárðr comes to him in his dream, calls him a traitor to the faith of his ancestors and places his hands on his eyes. Gestr awakens with a horrible eye pain and dies soon after, in his baptismal clothes. The mainly benevolent guardian spirit Bárðr demonstrates thus in his last appearance how dangerous he can also be."[177]

Bárðr had become "þögull ok illr viðskiptis" by this point after the disappearance of his daughter Helga,[178] after which he kills his own nephews and wounds his brother: "This is explained [in] the saga not only by his sorrow but also by his upbringing and his parentage: *þat var meir ætt hans at vera í stórum hellum en húsum, því at hann fæddist upp með Dofra í Dofrafjöllum; var hann tröllum ok líkari at afli ok vexti en mennskum mönnum.*"[179] This is followed in the saga by: "Varð hann og mörgum hin mesta bjargvættur",[180] which serves to explain his supernatural ability to be summoned in times of need, to which Ármann adds:

Within the framework of the saga, the explanation seems

---

[177] Ármann Jakobsson. 2006, 3-4.

[178] Bárðar saga Snæfellsáss 1986, ch. 6.

[179] Ármann Jakobsson. 2006, 5. **Translation for the quote:** "His family was more likely to live in large caves than in houses, as he had been raised by Dofri in the Dovrefjell. He was also more like trolls in strength and size than like human beings (Bard's saga 1997, 244.)

[180] Bárðar saga Snæfellsáss 1986, ch. 6. **Translation:** For many he also proved to be a source of real help in need (Bard's saga 1997, 244.)

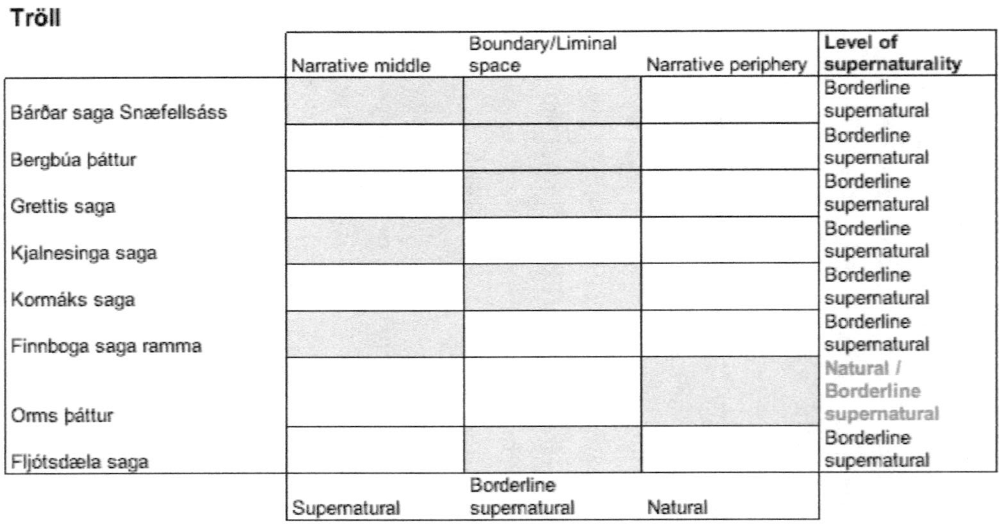

Tröll

	Narrative middle	Boundary/Liminal space	Narrative periphery	Level of supernaturality
Bárðar saga Snæfellsáss				Borderline supernatural
Bergbúa þáttur				Borderline supernatural
Grettis saga				Borderline supernatural
Kjalnesinga saga				Borderline supernatural
Kormáks saga				Borderline supernatural
Finnboga saga ramma				Borderline supernatural
Orms þáttur				Natural / Borderline supernatural
Fljótsdæla saga				Borderline supernatural
	Supernatural	Borderline supernatural	Natural	

Figure 10: Tröll in Íslendingasögur

plausible enough. The very need for it suggests, though,
that Bárðr is an ambiguous figure, at the same time human
and not quite human — and the difference is at least partly
defined by his dwellings. Whereas giants and trolls may
live in mountains, Bárðr had hitherto been a part of the
human world, so that people had perhaps forgotten his
fostering. The ambiguity of Bárðr is perhaps the main
theme of the first six chapters of Bárðar saga, and reflected
in his ambiguous parentage, his constant moving between
the world of men and the world of ogres. It is perhaps also
reflected in his role after his disappearance: he becomes a
guardian spirit and defender of the region, whom ordinary
humans may summon in their hour of need.[181]

Thus Bárðr has some superhuman abilities yet is human up until
the point he decidedly turns into a tröll.[182] Bárðr is descended from
Dumbshaf but settles in Iceland, which is the narrative centerpoint
of the saga whereas Dumbshaf remains on the periphery; he then
relocates into the mountains and is only ever seen since as a nature
spirit, neither good nor evil. He seems to fit naturally within the realm
of the possible within the saga, yet he possesses abilities unheard of
among mortal men. From this it is evident that Bárðr fits the definition
of tröll perfectly.

Ármann Jakobsson argues that to the "author of Bárðar saga, Bárðr
was as much a part of the past as Snorri goði was to the author of
Eyrbyggja [...] Our belief in the accuracy or probability of Bárðar
saga should thus have no effect on whether it is classified as a work of
history or fiction. Its inclusion in Vatnshyrna indicates on the contrary

---

[181] Ármann Jakobsson. 2006, 5.
[182] Ármann Jakobsson. 2006, 4.

that, like other Icelandic Family Sagas, it was indeed to all intents and purposes an historical work",[183] to which I heartily agree: there is no indication that the legend of Bárðr Snæfellsás was thought to be fictional. These will be the final words on Bárðar saga Snæfellsáss for the time being.

There is a considerable amount of fear for tröll in *Grettis saga*. The first mention of tröll in the saga is after Grettir kills Skeggi and jokes in verse about it having been a tröll.[184] In chapter 33 a shepherd goes missing from the farmer Þórhallr who has had to deal with the *aptrgangr* of another shepherd of his who was killed:

> Veðr var heldr kalt ok fjúk mikit. Því var Þorgautr vanr,
> at koma heim, þá er hálfrøkkvat var, en nú kom hann ekki
> heim í þat mund. Kómu tíðamenn, sem vant var. Þegar
> þótti mǫnnum eigi ólíkt á horfask sem fyrr. Bóndi vildi
> láta leita eptir sauðamanni, en tíðamenn tǫlðusk undan ok
> sǫgðusk eigi mundu hætta sér út í trollahendr um nætr,
> ok treystisk bóndi eigi at fara, ok varð ekki af leitinni.[185]

It is later resolved that the second shepherd was not killed by tröll but by the afturganga of another shepherd previously gone missing, Glámr. We shall return to him later. In a few instances, Grettir himself

---

[183]Ármann Jakobsson. 1998, 55.

[184]Grettis saga Ásmundarsonar 1936, ch. 16.

[185]Grettis saga Ásmundarsonar 1936, 33. **Translation:** The weather was fairly cold, and the snow was drifting heavily. Thorgaut was accustomed to come back at twilight, but on this occasion he did not return at that time. People returned from the mass as usual and thought events were following a familiar pattern. The farmer wanted to mount a search for his shepherd, but the people who had returned from mass argued against it, saying they would not risk being snatched away by trolls in the night. The farmer did not have the resolve to go out himself, so nothing came of the search (The saga of Grettir the strong 1997, 103)

is likened to tröll. In chapter 38:

> Grettir ræðr nú inn í húsit ok vissi eigi, hverir fyrir váru.
> Kuflinn var sýldr allr, þegar hann kom á land, ok var hann
> furðu mikill tilsýndar, sem troll væri. Þeim, sem fyrir váru,
> brá mjǫk við þetta, ok hugðu, at óvættr myndi vera.[186]

In chapter 57:

> Þá mælti Þórir: „Þat hefi ek spurt," sagði hann, „at Grettir
> væri afbragðsmaðr fyrir hreysti sakar ok hugar, en þat
> vissa ek aldri, at hann væri svá fjǫlkunnigr, sem nú sé ek,
> því at þar falla hálfu fleiri, sem hann horfir bakinu við; nú
> sé ek, at hér er við troll at eiga, en ekki við menn."[187]

In chapter 64, Þorsteinn hvíti and his wife Steinvǫr at Sandhaugar are
introduced to the saga, and it is expressed that "Þar þótti mǫnnum
reimt mjǫk sakar trǫllagangs".[188] One evening Þorsteinn goes missing:

> Lǫgðusk menn niðr til svefns um kveldit; ok um nóttina
> heyrðu menn brak mikit í skálann ok til sængr bónda:

---

[186] Grettis saga Ásmundarsonar 1936, ch. 38. **Translation:** Grettir burst into the house,
unaware who was inside. By the time he reached land his cowl was frozen stiff, and he
looked frighteningly huge, like a troll. The people inside were startled and took him to
be an evil creature (The saga of Grettir the strong 1997, 111.)

[187] Grettis saga Ásmundarsonar 1936, 57. **Translation:** Then Thorir said, "I have heard
that Grettir was exceptionally strong and brave but I never knew he was skilled in the
magic arts until what I have seen now. Twice as many men are being killed while he
keeps his back turned to them. I see now that we are dealing with a troll, not a man."
(The saga of Grettir the strong 1997, 138.)

[188] Their farm was haunted by trolls (The saga of Grettir the strong 1997, 151.). The
Old Norse text does not imply that the farm was indeed haunted by trolls, as trolls in
general do not haunt farms; the word 'trǫllagangr' here means that the cause of the
haunting is not known, but it is thought to be draugar, not tröll.

engi þorði upp at standa at forvitnask um, því at þar var

fámennt mjǫk. Húsfreyja kom heim um morgininn, ok var

bóndi horfinn, ok vissi engi, hvat af honum var orðit.[189]

Later, Steinvǫr convinces one of the farmhands to stay at home while
she goes to mass; in light of the previous event, he is reluctant but
stays home anyway. He subsequently disappears and they find traces
of blood in the entrance to the farm house. Grettir receives word that
óvættir had taken both Þorsteinn and the farmhand, and as "honum
var mjǫk lagit at koma af reimleikum eða aptrgǫngum, þá gerði hann
ferð sína til Bárðardals ok kom atfangadag jóla til Sandhauga." It
follows that "Hann dulðisk ok nefndisk Gestr. Húsfreyja sá, at hann
var furðu mikill vexti, en heimafólk var furðu hrætt við hann; hann
beiddisk þar gistingar."[190]

Again he is likened to a tröll in this passage as he seems to large
to be human, and then yet again, as soon after he carries Steinvǫr
and her daughter over a river which is impassable due to the spring
jökulhlaups. The passage over is extremely dangerous and the women
dare not scream out of terror; Grettir in the guise of Gestr then literally
tosses the women on to the bank on the other side and turns back
immediately. When Steinvǫr reaches her destination she is asked how

---

[189]Grettis saga Ásmundarsonar 1936, ch. 64. **Translation:** Everyone went to bed that
evening, and in the night a great crashing noise was heard in the main room, moving
in the direction of the farmer's bed. No one dared to get out of bed and find out what
it was, because there were very few people there. When his wife came home in the
morning the farmer had vanished and no one knew what had come of him (The saga
of Grettir the strong 1997, 151.)

[190]Grettis saga Ásmundarsonar 1936, ch. 64. **Translation:** because he was particularly
skilful at putting an end to hauntings and ghosts he set off for Bardardal, arriving at
Sandhaugar on Christmas Eve. He went in disguise and called himself Gest (Visitor).
The farmer's wife could see that he was exceptionally powerfully built, but the other
people who lived there were afraid of him. He asked to be allowed to stay there.

she got there, to which she replies that she does not know "hvárt hana hefði yfir flutt maðr eða troll."[191] When Grettir returns to Sandhólar he encounters a *trollkona* in the living room who proceeds to attack him:

> Hon var sterkari, en hann fór undan kœnliga, en allt þat, sem fyrir þeim varð, brutu þau, jafnvel þverþilit undan stofunni. Hon dró hann fram yfir dyrnar ok svá í anddyrirt; þar tók hann fast í móti. Hon vildi draga hann út ór bœnum, en þat varð eigi, fyrr en þau leystu frá allan útiduraumbúninginn ok báru hann út á herðum sér; þœfði hon þá ofan til árinnar ok allt fram at gljúfrum. Þá var Gestr ákafliga móðr, en þó varð annathvárt at gera, at herða sik, ella myndi hon steypa honum í gljúfrin. Alla nóttina sóttusk þau. Eigi þóttisk hann hafa fengizk við þvílíkan ófagnað fyrir afls sakar. Hon hafði haldit honum svá fast at sér, at hann mátti hvárigri hendi taka til nǫkkurs, útan hann helt um hana miðja, kvinnuna; ok er þau kómu á árgljúfrit, bregðr hann flagðkonunni til sveiflu. Í því varð honum laus in hœgri hǫndin; hann þreif þá skjótt til saxins, er hann var gyrðr með, ok bregðr því, hǫggr þá á ǫxl trollinu, svá at af tók hǫndina hœgri, ok svá varð hann lauss, en hon steypðisk í gljúfrin ok svá í forsinn.[192]

---

[191]Grettis saga Ásmundarsonar 1936, ch. 64. **Translation:** whether it was a man or a troll who had carried her across.

[192]Grettis saga Ásmundarsonar 1936, ch. 65. **Translation:** She was stronger but he dodged her cleverly. They smashed everything that was in their way, even the partition which divided the room crossways. She dragged him out through the door and towards the front door, where he made a firm stand against her. She wanted to drag him outside the farmhouse, but could not manage it until they had broken down the entire door-frame and took it with them around their necks. Then she lugged him

It is interesting that the priest does not believe his story, yet it is also said that the people of Bárðardalr maintain the legend that the trollkona was petrified by the sun during their fight, and that she had cracked when he lopped off her arm and still stands there in woman shape on top of the cliff. When Grettir proposes to the priest that he prove his story by venturing into a cavern behind the waterfall down in the gorge, he encounters a jǫtunn who is "ógurliga mikill" and "hræðiligr at sjá":[193]

> En er Grettir kom at honum, hljóp jǫtunninn upp ok greip
> flein einn ok hjó til þess, er kominn var [. . .] Grettir hjó
> á móti með saxinu, ok kom á skaptit, svá at í sundr tók.
> Jǫtunninn vildi þá seilask á bak sér aptr til sverðs, er þar
> hekk í hellinum. Í því hjó Grettir framan á brjóstit, svá
> at náliga tók af alla bringspelina ok kviðinn, svá at iðrin
> steypðusk ór honum ofan í ána, ok keyrði þau ofan eptir
> ánni. Ok er prestr sat við festina, sá hann, at slyðrur
> nǫkkurar rak ofan eptir strengnum, blóðgar allar [. . .] Nú
> er frá Gretti at segja; hann lét skammt hǫggva í milli, þar
> til er jǫtunninn dó.[194]

off down to the river, right up to the chasm. Gest was exhausted, but either had to brace himself or let her hurl him into it. They struggled all night and he felt he had never fought such a powerful beast before. She was pressing him so tightly to her body that he could do nothing with either of his arms except clutch at her waist. When they were on the edge of the chasm he lifted her off her feet and swung her off balance, freeing his right arm. At once he grabbed for the short sword he was wearing, drew it, swung it at her shoulder and chopped off her right arm. He was released the moment she plunged into the chasm and under the waterfall (The saga of Grettir the strong 1997, 152-3.)

[193] The saga of Grettir the strong 1997, 154. "Monstrous in size and terrible to behold"

[194] Grettis saga Ásmundarsonar 1936, ch. 66. **Translation:** When Grettir approached it, the giant snatched up a pike and swung a blow at the intruder [. . .] Grettir returned the blow with his short-sword, striking the shaft and chopping through it. The giant

After this it is said that aptrgǫngr or reimleikar were never a problem in the vale since, and that Grettir had proved that his story was true.[195]

A central element to this saga is that of the unknown. Strange events seem to be taking place all around and people do not know what is causing them to happen, although their usual explanation is that they are the doing of tröll. When people go missing, the culprit is never seen, but it attacks people in their homes which is highly unusual even for tröll. Grettir himself is likened to a tröll several times for the reason that he is unusually large and menacing in the eyes of the people he interacts with. As with Þórir járnskjöldr, Grettir is considered a tröll until identified, after which he ceases to be a tröll.[196]

The two tröll Grettir fights[197] are not of the same kind. The *trollkona* is a strong adversary and it is said that they fight all through the night until Grettir can make his move to finish her off. His story is not believed until he has killed a second tröll, a *jǫtunn*, whom he finds in a cave behind the waterfall where the trollkona fell, but after that it is accepted as truth. Their whereabouts are located on the other side of a figurative liminal space, i.e. in a cave behind the waterfall in a barely accessible gorge. The jǫtunn is either not as tough as the trollkona or Grettir simply had a better advantage when fighting him. Both tröll fit well in with the hypothesis as they are hard but possible to believe

---

tried to reach behind him for a sword that was hanging on the wall of the cave, but as he did so Grettir struck him on the breast, sclicing his lower ribs and belly straight off and sending his innards gushing out into the river where they were swept away. The priest, sitting by the rope, saw some slimy, bloodstained strands floating in the current [. . .] To turn to Grettir, he struck a few quick blows at the giant until he was dead (The saga of Grettir the strong 1997, 154.)

[195] Grettis saga Ásmundarsonar 1936, ch. 67.

[196] Cf. Ármann Jakobsson. 2009b, 192-3.

[197] Not counting Glámr, who I think fits better in with draugar.

in and they both live in a cave; the world view of the saga's characters is adapted to their verified existence as they leave the realm of the *unknown*, whereas before the word tröll was only used in a general way to describe the *unexplained* phenomena (which, as discussed in 3.1, would be in accordance with Todorov's definition of fantastic phenomena). Both the tröll in *Grettis saga* are marked in a single cell in the table above.

In Kormáks saga, Kormákr is waging war in Scotland when a blótrisi[198] emerges from the woods:

> ok tóksk þar atgangr harðr. Kormákr var ósterkari, en
> risinn trollauknari. Kormákr leit til sverðs síns, ok var
> rennt ór slíðrum. Kormákr seildisk til ok hjó risann banahǫgg.
> Risinn lagði þó svá fast hendr at síðum Kormáks, at rifin
> brotnuðu, ok fell Kormákr ok risinn dauðr ofan á hann, ok
> komsk Kormákr eigi upp.[199]

The encounter takes place in Scotland, which could count as a second narrative middle. The blótrisi however emerges from the woods which is clearly a liminal space. He is more powerful than Kormákr

---

[198]This is the only instance where a 'blótrisi' is ever mentioned in the literature. Einar Ól. Sveinsson hypothesises that it is supposed to symbolize some Celtic notion, possibly a druid (Kormáks saga: 299). Based on the description I find this rather unlikely; 'blót' could rather refer to the risi having been conjured up, like e.g. the golem in Jewish folklore. Rory McTurk translates this to "a giant whom the Scots worshipped as an idol", (The Complete Sagas of Icelanders I: 223) which although I disagree with is likelier than it being a druid.

[199]Kormáks saga 1939, ch. 27. **Translation:** and a bitter struggle ensued. Of the two, Kormak was the weaker; the giant had more of a troll's strength. Kormak felt for his sword, but it had slipped from its scabbard. Kormak stretched out his hand for it and struck the giant his deathblow. The giant gripped Kormak's sides so firmly, however, that his ribs broke, and Kormak fell with the dead giant on top of him, and could not get up (Kormak's saga 1997, 223.)

as the trollkona is in *Grettis saga*, yet Kormákr is quick to dispatch
him, suffering a broken ribcage from their fight which leads to his
death. This incident is treated as if nothing out of the ordinary has
happened, and mostly his friends mourn "er hann skyldi svá óvarliga
farit hafa",[200] as if he received his injuries by being clumsy. What is
most important here is that the encounter with the blótrisi seems to
be understood as a genuine possibility in Scotland. This narrative is
also in approval of the hypothesis.

In Fljótsdæla saga, Þorvaldr rescues Droplaug from a cave in Hjalt-
land[201] where a jötunn has held her captive:

> Ok í þessu stígr jötunninn upp í skorina bjargsins, þá sem
> Þorvaldr hafði sét, en öðrum fæti á flesin, ok varð hann eigi
> vótskór. Ok sá hann, at til þess var þessi skor, at jötunninn
> vildi eigi vaða. En í þessu kemr Þorvaldr at ok hleypr inn
> undir hann, en jötunninn breiðir frá sér lámana, ok ætlaði
> at taka Þorvald. En í því höggr Þorvaldr til hans, ok kom á
> mitt lærit jötunsins, ok tók af fótinn vinstra fyrir ofan kné,
> en hinn hægra fyrir neðan kné, ok kom sverðit í sandinn
> niðr.

This victory seems easy enough, but then the jötunn speaks:

> „Illa hefir þú mik svikit ok meir en ek ætlaða, at þú hefir
> tekit þat eitt vópn, er mér mátti grand vinna. Fór ek af því
> óhræddr eptir þér, at ek hugsaða ekki, at smámenni mundi
> mér verða at bana. En nú muntu þykjast hafa mikinn sigr
> unnit. Muntu ætla at bera vópn þetta ok þínir ættmenn.
> En þat mæli ek um, at þá verði þeim sízt gagn at, er mest

---

[200]Kormak's saga 1997, 223. "acted so imprudently"
[201]Shetland.

liggr við." Þorvaldr leitaði þess á, at hann skyldi ekki fleiri
orð mæla þeim til óþurftar, ok höggr á hálsinn, svó at af
tók höfuðit, og stakk höfðinu milli þjóanna.[202]

The jötunn's prophecy is of course fulfilled during the course of the
saga. It is interesting that Þorvaldr sticks the jötunn's head between
his buttocks after having cut it off, as it is a common measure to ward
themselves from the murdered returning as an afturganga, and this
is seldom done to tröll. Again, we see that the tröll in question lives
in a liminal space abroad, in a cave; it is larger and stronger than an
ordinary human being and possesses some supernatural qualities, in
this case either the gift of foresight or the ability to curse items such
as the sword. The jötunn of *Fljótsdæla saga* also fits the hypothesis.

Both *Kjalnesinga saga* and *Finnboga saga ramma* include a fight between their respective protagonist and a blámaðr. In *Kjalnesinga saga*,
Rauðr warns Búi that king Haraldr will "etja á þig því trölli, er ek veit
mest í Nóregi, en þat er blámaðr sá, er mörgum manni hefir at bana

---

[202] Fljótsdæla saga 1950, ch. 5. **Translation:** At that moment the giant stepped up into
the cleft in the cliff which Thorvald had seen before, and he put the other foot on the flat
rock, and he did not get his shoe wet. And he saw that the cleft was there because the
giant did not want to wade the shoal water. At that moment Thorvald came up and ran
in underneath him, and the giant spread out his paws intending to catch Thorvald. But
at that moment Thorvald struck him and the blow landed on the middle of the giant's
thigh and took off the left leg above the knee and the right one below the knee, and the
sword came down in the sand [. . .] "You have betrayed me wickedly, and worse than I
thought, because you took from me the only weapon which could do me injury. That's
why I came after you without any fear, because I had no idea that a puny human would
turn out to be my killer. Now you must think that you have won a great victory. You
will be thinking that you and your descendants will bear this weapon. But I lay a curse
on it, so that it will be the least help to them when they most depend on it." Thorvald
wanted to stop him saying anything else to harm them, and struck at his neck so that
the head came off, and he placed the head between the giant's thighs (The saga of the
people of Fljotsdal 1997, 387-8.)

106

orðit."[203] Sure enough: "Konungr lét þá leiða fram blámanninn, ok héldu á honum fjórir menn. Hann grenjaði fast ok lét tröllsliga."[204] When Búi asks where the man is he is intended to fight, the king points to the blámaðr, to which Búi replies that "Ekki sýnist mér þat maðr. Trölli sýnist mér þat líkara:"[205] The blámaðr is then released upon the fighting field:

> Eftir þat gekk Búi fram á völlinn, ok er fólkit sá hann, þá mæltu margir, at þat væri illa, er trölli skyldi etja upp á jafndrengiligan mann. Þeir létu þá lausan blámanninn. Hljóp hann þá grenjandi at Búa. Ok er þeir mættust, tókust þeir afar fast ok skiptust. Skildi Búi þat skjótt, at hann var mjök aflvani fyrir þessu kykvendi. Forðaði hann sér þá við föllum, en stóð þó fast ok fór undan víða um völlinn [...] En er þeir höfðu at gengizt um stund, þá mæddist blámaðrinn ákafliga, ok tók at láta í honum sem þá at lætr í göltum, þá er þeir gangast at, ok á þann hátt felldi hann froðu. Ok er Búi fann þat, lét hann hörfast undan at hellunni. Blámaðrinn herti þá at at nýju, ok váru ógurlig hans læti at heyra, því at hann var drjúgum sprunginn af sókn. En er Búi kom at hellunni, svá at hann kenndi hennar með hælunum, þá herti blámaðrinn at, slíkt er hann mátti. Búi brá þá við, er minnst var ván, ok hljóp hann þá öfugr yfir hellina, en blámanninum urðu lausar

---

[203]"turn loose against you the greatest troll in the whole of Norway. It's a black creature which has killed many men" (The saga of the people of Kjalarnes 1997, 322.)

[204]The king had the black man brought out. Four men were holding him back. He was howling out loud and carrying on just like a troll. (The saga of the people of Kjalarnes 1997, 323.)

[205]"That doesn't look like a man to me. It looks more like a troll" (The saga of the people of Kjalarnes 1997, 323.)

hendrnar ok skruppu af fangastakkinum. Búi kippti þá at
sér blámanninum, slíkt er hann mátti. Hrataði hann þá at
hellunni, svá at bringspalir hans tóku þar, sem hvössust
var. Þá hljóp Búi ofan á hann með öllu afli. Gengu þá í
sundr bringspalirnir í blámanninum, ok því næst var hann
dauðr.[206]

The only part of this whole description hinting at the blámaðr resembling a human being is the suffix -*maðr* meaning man. He is referred to
as a tröll and his frothing and panting is likened to hogs. The blámaðr
is stronger than Búi, but neither as quick nor as smart as he is. What
is peculiar in this narrative is that the blámaðr is the property of king
Haraldr and used as a wrestler for his entertainment. Nevertheless
he is in all respects a tröll, albeit in captivity at the king's court.

---

[206]Kjalnesinga saga 1986, ch. 15. **Translation:** Then Bui went out on the field, and
when the people saw him, many of them said how shameful it was that a troll should
be matched against such a fine figure of a man. Then the black man was released. He
ran towards Bui, howling. When they met they clashed hard and wrestled. Bui quickly
saw that he was inferior in strength to this creature. He managed to avoid a fall, but
remained on his feet and backed away all round the field. Bui realised that his bones
would have been broken if the clothes had not protected him. Then he noticed that the
black man was trying to get him to the stone. When they had been fighting for a long
while, the black man grew very tired and began grunting the way hogs do when they
fight, and began to froth and foam. When Bui noticed this, he backed up towards the
stone. The black man renewed his efforts then, and it was terrible to hear his noises,
because he was almost dead [I would say 'very tired'] from the fighting. When Bui
reached the stone and could feel it with his heels, the black man pushed as hard as he
could. Bui did what was least expected and jumed backwards over the stone, and the
black man lost the hold that he had on the wrestling jacket. Bui tugged the black man
towards him as hard as he could, tumbling him onto the stone so that his ribcage hit the
sharpest point. Then Bui jumped down on him with all his strength. The black man's
ribcage broke apart and he was dead on the spot (The saga of the people of Kjalarnes
1997, 323-4.)

Very much the same happens in *Finnboga saga*, where Hákon jarl summons Finnbogi to wrestle with a blámaðr, adding that "Þarftu ekki at hlífast við, því at ekki skal hann hlífa þér."[207] Their fight however does not last as long as when Búi fights his blámaðr:

> Finnbogi sá hjá stólinum, hvar stóð einn blámaðr, ok þóttist hann eigi hafa sét leiðiligra mann. Síðan bjuggust þeir til glímu, ok varð sá atgangr bæði harðr ok langr. Þóttist Finnbogi þat sjá, at þessi var magnaðr ekki lítt. Steinn stóð á vellinum harðla mikill, ok þar vildi hann færa Finnboga at. Hann lét þá berast at steininum, ok er þeir kómu at, þá snarast Finnbogi frá ok gengr hann á bak aftr blámanninn ok setr hrygg hans á steininn ok brýtr sundur.[208]

Finnbogi almost seems bored by the blámaðr before they fight. It is implied that the blámaðr is very strong as they wrestle for a long while, which then ends when Finnbogi tricks the blámaðr and then calmly breaks his back on a rock lying in the field. The same applies to this narrative as the one in *Kjalnesinga saga*: the tröll is held in captivity so it resides within the narrative middle, but in all respects it is nevertheless a tröll. Both narratives support the hypothesis.

Finally I will look at two Íslendingaþættir for comparison, *Orms*

---

[207]Finnboga saga ramma 1986, ch. 16. **Translation:** You won't need to hold back, because he won't spare you (The saga of Finnbogi the mighty 1997, 238.)

[208]Finnboga saga ramma 1986, ch. 16. **Translation:** Finnbogi saw that the black man was standing beside the chair, and he thought that he had never seen anyone more hideous. They began to wrestle and the contest was both long and hard. Finnbogi felt sure that his opponent was strengthened not a little by magic spells. A huge rock stood in the field, and the black man wanted to carry Finnbogi over to it. Finnbogi allowed himself to be brought there, and when they reached it he swiftly turned around and knocked the black man backwards, set his spine against the rock, and broke it asunder (The saga of Finnbogi the mighty 1997, 238.)

þáttr Stórólfssonar and *Bergbúa þáttr*. In *Bergbúa þáttr*, Þórðr and his
farmhand go to mass. A snowstorm hits them and they lose their
way, so they walk up a steep cliff and come upon a cave. But they are
not alone: "En á fyrsta þriðjungi nætr þá höfðu þeir heyrt, at nökkut
fór innar eftir hellinum ok útar at þeim."[209]

They hear a great noice deeper within the cave and when they
look into the darkness they spot what seems to them to be two full
moons; these are the eyes of their host, who speaks to them in verse
once every third part of the night, reciting pagan mythology. The
voice in the cave then warns them that bad things will befall them if
they do not remember the poem. At daybreak, Þórðr makes sure to
touch with his foot the mark of a cross he had made in the entrance
to the cave. While he remembers the whole poem, his farmhand does
not remember a single word of it:

> En ári síðar eftir þetta færði Þórðr byggð sína nær kirkju,
> en at jafnlengd þessa atburðar önnur misseri þá andaðist
> húskarl, förunautr Þórðar. En hann lifði lengi síðan, ok
> urðu honum engir hlutir kynligar en áðr, en þó eru slíkt
> fáheyrðir hlutir.[210]

The voice's owner is never seen, but it most assuredly is a tröll. Like
Bárðr Snæfellsás it is of pagan ancestry, and like many other tröll it
lives in a cave and either has the power of foresight or the ability to

---

[209]Bergbúa þáttr 1986, 392. **Translation:** But during the first third of the night they
heard something moving inside along the cave passage and coming out toward them
(The tale of the mountain-dweller 1997, 444.)

[210]Bergbúa þáttr 1986, 400. **Translation:** In the following year Thord moved his farm
closer to the church, and exactly one year later the farmhand who had accompanied
Thord died. But Thord lived for a long time after that, and nothing more peculiar ever
happened to him; though this event was peculiar enough (The tale of the mountain-
dweller 1997, 447-8.)

curse people; its prophecy comes true as Þórðr's farmhand, who did not remember the verse, dies following the encounter.

The tröll Brúsi in *Orms þáttr* (also called jötunn) also lives in a cave. When Ásbjörn seeks him out to kill him he fails:

> En Ásbjörn gengr þar til, er hann kemr at hellinum Brúsa, ok snarar þegar inn í. Honum var nökkut dimmt fyrir augum, en skuggamikit var í hellinum. Hann verðr eigi fyrr varr við en hann er þrifinn á loft ok færðr niðr svá hart, at Ásbirni þótti furða í. Verðr hann þess þá varr, at þar er kominn Brúsi jötunn, ok sýndist heldr mikilligr. Brúsi mælti þá: „Þó lagðir þú mikit kapp á at sækja hingat. Skaltu nú ok erendi hafa, því at þú skalt hér lífit láta með svá miklum harmkvölum, at þat skal aðra letja at sækja mik heim með ófriði." Fletti hann þá Ásbjörn klæðum, því at svá var þeira mikill aflamunr, at jötunninn varð einn at ráða þeira í milli [. . .] Síðan opnaði Brúsi kvið á Ásbirni ok náði þarmaenda hans ok knýtti um járnsúluna ok leiddi Ásbjörn þar í hring um. En Ásbjörn gekk einart, ok rökðust svá á enda allir hans þarmar.[211]

[211] Orms þáttr Stórólfssonar 1986, ch. 7 **Translation:** Asbjorn walked on until he came to Brusi's cave and went straight inside. It was rather difficult for him to see, for it was shadowy in the cave. Before he knew it he was snatched up into the air and dashed down so hard that he was amazed. He perceived that this was the giant Brusi, who appeared to be rather large indeed. Brusi said, "You've put a lot of effort into coming here. It will not have been wasted, either, for here you shall lose your life in such intense agony that it will dissuade others from visiting me with hostile intent." He then stripped Asbjorn of his clothes, for so great was the difference in their strength that in their dealings the giant alone made all the decisions [. . .] Then Brusi opened up Asbjorn's belly and took hold of the end of his intestines, which he fastened to the iron column; then he led Asbjorn round and round, and Asbjorn kept going until his intestines had been wound out of him" (Orm Storolfsson's tale 1997, 461-2.)

Brúsi explicitly tells Ásbjörn that he will kill him to keep others from attempting to seek him out with ill intentions at his home, and Ásbjörn is powerless to stop him as Brúsi is immensely mighty. Soon after Ormr comes looking for Brúsi as well but finds his mother first, who is a *ketta*:

Hann gekk þá inn í hellinn ok lagði málajárn í dyrrnar. En er hann var inn kominn, sá hann, hvar kettan hljóp með gapanda ginit. Ormr hafði boga ok örvamæli. Lagði hann þá ör á streng ok skaut at kettunni þremr örum, en hon hendi allar með hváftunum ok beit í sundr. Hefir hon sig þá at Ormi ok rekr klærnar framan í fangit, svá at Ormr kiknar við, en klærnar gengu í gegnum klæðin, svá at í beini stóð. Hon ætlar þá at bíta í andlit Ormi. Finnr hann þá, at honum mun eigi veita, heitir þá á sjálfan guð ok inn heilaga Petrum postula at ganga til Róms, ef hann ynni kettuna ok Brúsa, son hennar. Síðan fann Ormr, at minnkaðist afl kettunnar. tekr hann þá annarri hendi um kverkar henni, en annarri um hrygg ok gengr hana á bak ok brýtr í sundr í henni hrygginn ok gengr svá af henni dauðri.[212]

[212]Orms þáttr Stórólfssonar 1986, ch. 9 **Translation:** He then went into the cave, laying an inlaid sword in the entrance. But when he had come inside he saw the ogress leap at him, her mouth agape. Orm had a bow and quiver. He fitted an arrow to his bowstring and let fly three arrows at the ogress, but she caught them all between her jaws and bit them in two. She then leapt upon Orm and dug her claws into his chest so that Orm fell to his knees and the claws went through his clothing and pierced his flest to the bone. She tried to bite Orm in the face. He then saw that things would not go well for him, and he vowed than to God himself and to St. Peter the Apostle that he would go on a pilgrimage to Rome if he could defeat the ogress and her son Brusi. Then Orm felt that the strength of the ogress diminished. He gripped her with one

The word *ketta* is synonymous with *tröllkona*, and in many respects this ketta is comparable to the trollkona in *Grettis saga*. Both are mindless monsters with immense strength, both live in a cave, and the protagonist has trouble defeating it. Ormr needs the strength of God to defeat the ketta, and in pledging to go on a pilgrimage to Rome he receives this strength and kills the ketta. Then he goes after Brúsi:

> Ormr sá þá, hvar bálkr stórr var um þveran hellinn. Hann gengr þá innar at, en er hann kemr þar, sér hann, at fleinn mikill kemr útar í gegnum bálkinn. Hann var bæði digr ok langr. Ormr grípr þá í móti fleininum ok leggr af út. Brúsi kippir þá at sér fleininum, ok var hann fastr, svá at hvergi gekk. Þat undraðist Brúsi ok gægðist upp yfir bálkinn. En er Ormr sér þat, þrífr hann í skeggit á Brúsa báðum höndum, en Brúsi bregzt við í öðrum stað. Sviptast þeir þá fast um bálkinn. Ormr hafði vafit skegginu um hönd sér ok rykkir til svá fast, at hann rífr af Brúsa allan skeggstaðinn, hökuna, kjaftana báða, vangafillurnar upp allt at eyrum. Gekk hér með holdit niðr at beini. Brúsi lét þá síga brýnnar ok grettisk heldr greppliga. Ormr stökkr þá innar yfir bálkinn. Grípast þeir þá til ok glíma lengi. Mæddi Brúsa þá fast blóðrás. Tekr hann þá heldr at ganga fyrir. Gefr Ormr þá á ok rekr Brúsa at bálkinum og brýtr hann þar um á bak aftr.[213]

hand on her throat and the other on her backbone and drove her over onto her back, snapped her backbone in two, and left her for dead (Orm Storolfsson's tale 1997, 465)

[213]Orms þáttr Stórólfssonar 1986, ch. 9. **Translation:** Orm saw where a great partition ran across the middle of the cave. He went further in and when he came to it he saw that a large pike came out through the partition. It was both thick and long. Orm gripped the pike and bent it. Brusi then jerked the pike back but it was stuck fast and wouldn't budge. This puzzled Brusi, and he peeped up over the partition. When Orm

All these narratives show a similar creature, and the ten examples of tröll are all consistent with the hypothesis. The tröll lives in or around a liminal space; the only exceptions to this are the two blámenn in the service of the king and the jarl in *Kjalnesinga saga* and *Finnboga saga ramma* respectively, as Bárðr Snæfellsás was not a tröll until he left human society. The other tröll all live in caves. All of the tröll have in common some superhuman properties such as immense strength and a large size, and they are all terrifying to look at. They are not human, but they are not supernatural either. They belong to the unrecognizable, the unknown, yet their existence is acknowledged and they therefore are a part of the saga world; they are *mirabilia* bordering on *miracula*.

3.4.3 Draugar

The term draugr is not altogether unproblematic as it is not the term given to the most famous of medieval draugar in Iceland, as we will see in the following examples. Draugar are sometimes also referred to as tröll, e.g. Þórólfr bægifótr who has previously been mentioned. In some cases the distinction between tröll and draugr can be difficult to make, such as Ögmundur Eyþjófsbani in Örvar-Odds saga who

saw this he grabbed hold of Brusi's beard with both hands while Brusi, for his part, pulled back the other way. They then pulled back and forth over the wall. Orm had wrapped the beard round his hand and pulled so hard that he tore away all the bearded part of Brusi's face – the chin, both jaws and the cheeks all the way up to the ears, and with it came all the flesh clear to the bone.Brusi knitted his brows and grimaced rather horribly. Orm then leapt over to the inner side of the partition. They took hold of each other and wrestled for a long time. Brusi quickly grew weak from loss of blood, and began to give ground. Orm then pressed on and forced Brusi toward the partition and bent him backwards over it [a better translation would be that he broke his back on it] (Orm Storolfsson's tale 1997, 465.)

can be argued to be either. Nevertheless there is no reason for a researcher to not use it as an umbrella term.[214] A reasonable amount has been written about draugar in later years[215] and I will be basing my observations in part on this research.

Regrettably there is not opportunity to take all that has been written on the subject into consideration at this point. As with the results of my analysis in the other categories, the results for the category of draugar is shown in the table below (*figure 11*).

As is clear from the table, most of the draugar in the Íslendingasögur match the given criteria and thereby support the hypothesis. I will now present my arguments for these results and as with my analysis of tröll I will start with the most complicated example: the *Fróðárundr* in *Eyrbyggja saga*.

Þórgunna at Fróðá passes away and shortly after her burial

> þá sá menn á veggþili hússins, at komit var tungl hálft; þat
> máttu allir menn sjá, þeir er í húsinu váru; þat gekk ǫfugt
> um húsit ok andsœlis. Þat hvarf eigi á brott, meðan menn
> sátu við elda. Þóroddr spurði Þóri viðlegg, hvat þetta
> myndi boða. Þórir kvað þat vera urðarmána;[216] „mun
> hér eptir koma manndauðr," segir hann. Þessi tíðendi bar
> þar við viku alla, at urðarmáni kom inn hvert kveld sem
> annat.[217]

---

[214] Ármann Jakobsson. 2010, 190-192.

[215] Most notably Ármann Jakobsson. 2009a, Ármann Jakobsson. 2010, Keyworth 2007, Vésteinn Ólason. 2003, Torfi H. Tulinius. 1999, and especially on the Fróðárundr Kjartan G. Ottósson. 1983.

[216] "Urðr" can either mean 'fate' or 'death' (Eyrbyggja saga: 145). Therefore the translation 'blood moon' would be better than the 'weird-moon' in the translation in footnote 217.

[217] Eyrbyggja saga 1935, ch. 52. **Translation:** when they saw on the room's wainscoting

What happens next is that a shepherd comes home feeling ill, the little
he speaks he does in a foul temper, and the people at the farm think
it is probable that he has been bewitched as he keeps to and talks to
himself. Two weeks into winter he dies and is buried at the church,
but soon:

> gerðusk reimleikar miklir. Þat var eina nótt, at Þórir við-
> leggr gekk út nauðsynja sinna ok frá durunum annan veg;
> ok er hann vildi inn ganga, sá hann, at sauðamaðr var
> kominn fyrir dyrrnar; vildi Þórir inn ganga, en sauðamaðr
> vildi þat víst eigi; þá vildi Þórir undan leita, en sauðamaðr
> sótti eptir ok fekk tekit hann ok kastaði honum heim at
> durunum; honum varð illt við þetta, ok komsk þó til rúms
> síns ok var víða orðinn kolblár. Af þessu tók hann sótt
> ok andaðisk; var hann ok grafinn þar at kirkju; sýndusk
> þeir báðir jafnan síðan í einni ferð, sauðamaðr ok Þórir
> viðleggr; ok af þessu varð fólkit allt óttafullt, sem ván var.
> Eptir andlát Þóris tók sótt húskarl Þórodds ok lá þrjár nætr,
> áðr hann andaðisk; síðan dó hverr at ǫðrum, þar til er sex
> váru látnir[218]

that a half-moon had appeared. Everyone in the room could see it. It went backwards
around the house, against the motion of the sun. It did not disappear as long as people
were sitting in front of the fire. Thorodd asked Thorir Wood-leg what it might mean.
Thorir said it was a weird-moon, "and it will be followed by someone's death here,"
he said. This kept happening there all week, the weird-moon appearing every evening
just like the night before (The saga of the people of Eyri 1997, 199-200.)

[218]Eyrbyggja saga 1935, ch. 53 **Translation:** serious hauntings began. One night
Thorir Wood-leg went outside when nature called and was on his way back to the door,
but when he tried to go back inside, he saw that the shepherd was standing in front of
the doorway. Thorir wanted to go in, but the shepherd certainly did not want him to.
Then Thorir tried to get away, but the shepherd went after him and took hold of him
and threw him back against the door. He was hurt, but managed to get back to his bed,

Draugar

	Narrative middle	Boundary/Liminal space	Narrative periphery	Level of supernaturality
Eyrbyggja saga				Supernatural
Flóamanna saga				Supernatural
Grettis saga				Supernatural
Grænlendinga saga				Supernatural
Laxdæla saga				Supernatural
Brennu-Njáls saga				Supernatural
Færeyinga saga				Supernatural
Svarfdæla saga				Supernatural
Vatnsdæla saga				Supernatural
	Supernatural	Borderline supernatural	Natural	

Figure 11: Draugar in Íslendingasögur

As in many cases of hauntings, it is uncertain what catalyzes the undead return of the shepherd.[219] Þórir viðleggr, who prophesized that many deaths would follow the urðarmáni, gets infected by the shepherds supernatural disease and dies; consequently their afturgöngur are always seen together, and more people start dying. Shortly before Christmas while farmer Þóroddr is out collecting his dried fish, the head of a seal emerges from the fire in the grove on the floor. A servant beats the seal with a club, but it only raises itself higher from the grove, peeking up at the bed of the deceased Þórgunna. A farmhand resumes beating the seal, but this only seems to encourage it even more, causing the farmhand to faint which terrifies everyone. The young boy Kjartan then grabs a sledgehammer and bashes the seal in the head until it has disappeared down the floor again and Kjartan has hammered the floor together over its head, "ok svá fór jafnan um vetrinn, at allir fyrirburðir óttuðusk mest Kjartan."[220] But the haunting is not over yet:

> Um morguninn, er þeir Þóroddr fóru útan af Nesi með
> skreiðina, týndusk þeir allir út fyrir Enni; rak þar upp
> skipit ok skreiðina undir Ennit, en líkin fundusk eigi [. . .]
> En it fyrsta kveld, er menn váru at erfinu ok menn váru í
> sæti komnir, þá gengr Þóroddr bóndi í skálann ok fǫrunautar

black and blue all over. He became ill because of this, and died. He was buried there at the church. The shepherd and Thorir Wood-leg were always seen in each other's company after that. As might be expected, this terrified everyone. After Thorir's death one of Thorodd's farmhands became ill, and he lay in bed for three nights before dying. Then one after another died until six people had died altogether (The saga of the people of Eyri 1997, 200)

[219] E.g. Glámr's afturganga in Grettis saga.

[220] Eyrbyggja saga 1935, ch. 53 **Translation:** And so it wen on throughout the winter, with all the revenants fearing Kjartan the most (The saga of the people of Eyri 1997, 201)

hans allir alvátir. Menn fǫgnuðu vel Þóroddi, því at þetta
þótti góðr fyrirburðr, því at þá hǫfðu menn þat fyrir satt,
at þá væri mǫnnum vel fagnat at Ránar, ef sædauðir menn
vitjuðu erfis síns; en þá var enn lítt af numin forneskjan,[221]
þó at menn væri skírðir ok kristnir at kalla.[222]

Every night of the wake, Þóroddr and his companions return to the
feast to sit by the fire until it goes out. The people at Fróðá mistakenly
believe that they will stop coming after the wake is over; instead they
not only get Þóroddr and friends, they also receive Þórir viðleggr and
the six who died with him. The latter troup is covered in mud, which
they shake off all over Þóroddr and his company. The people at Fróðá
flee before this horrible scene and make their fire in another house,
and so it was for the duration of the Yuletide. The disturbances in the
stores where the dried fish is kept are also increasing:

> var þá svá at heyra nætr sem daga, at skreiðin væri rifin.
> Eptir þat váru þær stundir, at skreiðina þurfti at hafa; þar
> þá leitat til hlaðans, ok sá maðr, er upp kom á hlaðann,
> sá þau tíðendi, at upp or hlaðanum kom rófa, vaxin sem
> nautsrófa sviðin; hon var snǫgg ok selhár; sá maðr, er upp
> fór á hlaðann, tók í rófuna ok togaði ok bað aðra menn
> til fara með sér; fóru menn þá upp á hlaðann, bæði karlar

---

[221]It is interesting in itself that this condescending tone 'forneskja' is applied here
without questioning the validity of the haunting itself.

[222]Eyrbyggja saga 1935, ch. 54. **Translation:** On the first night of the funeral feast,
once everyone was in their seats, Thorodd the farmer and his companions came into
the fire room, completely drenched. People welcomed Thorodd warmly, thinking it
was a good omen, because at that time they believed that the drowned had been well
received by the sea-goddess Ran if they attended their own funeral feast. There was
still a small degree of belief in heathen ways, even though people had been babtised
and called themselves Christians (The saga of the people of Eyri 1997, 201)

ok konur, ok toguðu rófuna ok fengu eigi at gǫrt; skilðu
menn eigi annat en rófan væri dauð; ok er þeir toguðu
sem mest, strauk rófan ór hǫndum þeim, svá at skinnit
fylgði ór lófum þeira, er mest hǫfðu á tekit, en varð eigi
síðan vart við rófuna. Var þá skreiðin upp borin, ok var
þar hverr fiskr ór roði rifinn, svá at þar beið engan fisk í,
þegar niðr sótti í hlaðann, en þar fannsk engi hlutr kvikr
í hlaðanum. Næst þessum tíðendum tók sótt Þorgríma
galdrakinn, kona Þóris viðleggs; hon lá litla hríð, áðr hon
andaðisk, ok it sama kveld, sem hon var jǫrðuð, sásk hon í
liði með Þóri, bónda sínum. Þá endrnýjaði sóttina í annat
sinn, þá er rófan hafði sýnzk, ok ǫnduðusk þá meir konur
en karlar; létusk þá enn sex menn í hríðinni; en sumt
fólk flýði fyrir reimleikum ok aptrgǫngum. Um haustit
hǫfðu þar verit þrír tigir hjóna, en átján ǫnduðusk, en
fimm stukku í brottu, en sjau váru eptir at gói.[223]

---

[223]Eyrbyggja saga 1935, ch. 54. Góa is the fifth month of winter according to the old
Nordic calendar. It starts on a Sunday in the 18th week of winter, or the 18th to 24th
February. This indication of the elapsed time from autumn to late February is lacking
in the provided **translation:** night and day dried fish could be heard being torn up.
Then they reached the point when the dried fish needed to be used for meals, so they
went to look at the pile. The man who climbed up onto the pile saw that there was a tail
coming up through it, which was like a singed ox-tail, but it was short and covered in
seal-hair. The man at the top of the pile took hold of the tail and tugged at it, and then
asked other men to come up and help him. Both women and men climbed up onto the
pile, and tugged at the tail but they could not budge it. It did not occur to anyone that
the tail was anything but dead. But when they tugged their hardest, the tail stripped
the skin off the palms of the hands of those tugging hardest. Nothing was ever seen of
the tail again. The dried fish was then unpiled, and each fish in it had been ripped from
its skin so that there was no fish left right down through the pile, but there was also
nothing alive in the pile. The next thing that happened is that Thorir Wood-leg's wife,
Thorgrima Magiccheek, became ill. She lay in bed for a little while before she died,

At this time the inhabitants at Fróðá have had enough and the young Kjartan seeks the counsil of Snorri goði Þorgrímsson at Helgafell. Along with his son Þórðr kausi and six other men, Snorri sends the priest Gizurr hvíti with Kjartan to Fróðá and advices them to burn the bed sheets of Þórgunna "en sœkja þá menn alla í duradómi, er aptr gengu".[224] This ploy works, as the draugar of Þóroddr, the shepherd, Þórir viðleggr, Þórgunna and the others are all sentenced, to which they react by leaving one after the other. The farmhouses are then sanctioned with holy water "ok eptir þat tókusk af allar aptrgǫngr at Fróðá ok reimleikar"[225] and the hauntings are laid to rest once and for all.

There are several unique elements in this narrative. The cause of the Fróðárundr is for example one of a kind – that they happen because Þórgunna's bedsheets are not burnt posthumously as she had requested. To subpoena afturgöngur before a formal court is also unique, and the manner of exorcism is more Christian than in most medieval Icelandic narratives. The premonition is a rare element in ghost stories in Íslendingasögur, although hauntings sometimes serve in themselves the function of a premonition, and this is the only place

and the same evening that she was buried she was seen among her husband Thorir's company. Then there was a second wave of sickness that had come when the tail first appeared, and more women than men died. Six people die this time, and some people fled because of the hauntings and ghosts. In the autumn there had been thirty servants there, but eighteen had died and five had run away, so there were only seven left (The saga of the people of Eyri 1997, 201-202.)

[224]Eyrbyggja saga 1935, ch. 55. **Translation:** and all the revenants prosecuted at a door court (The saga of the people of Eyri 1997, 202.). According to the notes by Einar Ól. Sveinsson and Matthías Þórðarson, duradómr is a court called to by a prosecuter outside of a sanctioned þing or place of court. This is the only instance of such a court being assembled to deal with draugar (Eyrbyggja saga: 151).

[225]Eyrbyggja saga 1935, ch. 55. **Translation:** and after that all the revenants and ghosts left Froda (The saga of the people of Eyri 1997, 203)

in the Icelandic sagas where an urðarmáni appears. It is also unique that the dead cook for the living and a dried fish-eating, tailed creature is never mentioned in any other narrative.[226]

Kjartan G. Ottósson has postulated through von Sydow[227] that people are most susceptible to 'paranormal' experience when they are in a state of emotional shock, e.g. fear or anxiety, and that death can cause this sort of shock; it is strongest first after a person dies but then it lessens with time. It can become especially strong if the person died suddenly or violently, e.g. by drowning or suicide. In most ghost stories, the person who appears does so soon after dying, and usually they only appear to the people who were closest to them. Under such circumstances people can become afraid, especially if they are superstitious to begin with.[228] All of this can apply to the Fróðárundr. Psychological contemplations aside, belief in draugar, just as in tröll,[229] was common in medieval Iceland regardless,[230] and the fear that the dead would come back as afturgöngur does not seem to have changed from the writing time of Íslendingasögur until the 19th century,[231] in spite of being in opposition to the Christian world view. In other words: whereas demons and Hell were all very real things,[232] belief in draugar was a belief in the unsensible and the impossible, however common.

It is quite interesting to note that in the long narrative of the Fróðárundr, the sense of disbelief at what is happening is only re-

---

[226]Kjartan G. Ottósson. 1983, 9.

[227]von Sydow, C. W. "Övernaturliga väsen". Folketro. Nordisk kultur XIX. Stockholm 1935.

[228]Kjartan G. Ottósson. 1983, 13-14.

[229]Ármann Jakobsson. 1998, 55.

[230]Kjartan G. Ottósson. 1983, 19-20.

[231]Jón Hnefill Aðalsteinsson. 1988, Jón Árnason. 2003, 366-376.

[232]Kjartan G. Ottósson. 1983, 18.

alised once the afturgöngur have either shown acts of malice, been identified as evil, or in some other way outstayed their welcome, and with this disbelief comes fear. Þórir viðleggr is afraid of the shepherd's afturganga, who bars his entry to the building and then chases after him when he tries to escape it.[233] When Þóroddr and his companions enter the great hall of Fróðá, they are first greeted with rejoice! When it becomes evident that this is not a godly send, the sense of disbelief at the monstrosities in the great hall and the unthinkable need for exorcism becomes evident. The seal in the fire is instantly recognized as evil and therefore attacked; overall fear is evident in this part of the narrative. A sense of disbelief towards the singed tail in the fish storage is elementary to the story – they all are in search of a rational explanation for it, yet they have none. The macabre company seen roaming the countryside at night produces terror, and most of those surviving the hauntings flee Fróðá for good.

> Íslendingar hinir fornu höfðu hin margvíslegustu ráð gegn
> afturgöngum, og kaþólska kirkjan réð yfir ýmsum vop-
> num gegn illum vættum. Þær draugasögur sem ekki falla
> vel að þessum hugmyndakerfum eru fyrir þá sök mag-
> naðari en aðrar. Frásögnin af Fróðárundrum telst greini-
> lega til slíkra sagna. Ef draugasögurnar eru þess eðlis að
> lagður er trúnaður á þær, hvetur óhugnaðurinn sem af
> þeim stafar jafnframt til þess að leitað sé skýringa á því,
> hvernig á draugaganginum stóð, m.a. til þess að eiga ekki

---

[233]This is not the only narrative where a man is attacked by a draugur or a demon for having gone to the lavatory in the night; both draugar and demons are heavily associated with the carnal and not least the rear end (Ármann Jakobsson, 2010: 197-201), as with the act of cutting of the head of a dead body and sticking it in its rear. An example of the demon in the lavatory, cf. Þorsteins þáttr skelks.

á hættu að lenda í einhverju svipuðu.[234]

All this is evident in the narrative of Fróðárundr: this overwhelming
need to understand exactly what is happening so it can be stopped
and then prevented. These precautions however were not always as
potent as they should have been, as I explored earlier in this paper.
Þórólfr bægifótur in Eyrbyggja saga returned in spite of all the proper
arrangements being made, and he too desolates an entire region:

> Í þenna tíma bjó Þóroddr Þorbrandsson í Álptafirði; hann
> átti þá bæði londin, Úlfarsfell ok Ørlygsstaði, en þá var
> svá mikill gangr um aptrgongur Þórólfs bægifóts, at menn
> þóttusk eigi mega búa á londum þeim; en Bólstaðr var þá
> auðr, því at Þórólfr tók þegar aptr at ganga, er Arnkell var
> látinn, ok deyddi bæði menn ok fé þar á Bólstað; hefir ok
> engi maðr traust til borit at byggja þar fyrir þær sakar. En
> er þar var aleytt, sótti Bægifótr upp til Úlfarsfells ok gerði
> þar mikil vandræði; en allt fólk varð óttafullt, þegar vart
> varð við Bægifót.[235]

The whole community is affected by Þórólfr's haunting and almost
every farmstead is abandoned. An unnamed farmer says that it is
"ætlan manna, at Bægifótr myndi eigi fyrr létta en hann hefði eytt

---

[234]Kjartan G. Ottósson. 1983, 21.

[235]Eyrbyggja saga 1935, ch. 63. **Translation:** Thorodd Thorbrandsson was living at
Alftafjord this time, and he had estates at both Ulfarsfell and Orlygsstadir. Thorolf
Lame-foot's ghost had been so active that people did not think they could live on either
of these estates. Boldstad was now deserted, because Thorolf had begun to haunt it as
soon as Arnkel died, and both people and livestock had been killed there. No one had
dared to farm there after that happened. When it was derelict, Lame-foot moved up
to Ulfarsfell and caused a lot of trouble there. Everyone was terrified whenever they
caught sight of Lame-foot (The saga of the people of Eyri 1997, 211-212.)

allan fjǫrðinn bæði að mǫnnum ok fé, ef engra ráða væri í leitat".[236]
All in all, both narratives of Fróðárundr and of Þórólfr bægifótr adhere
to the principle of the hypothesis: they invoke disbelief, terror and
the encounters all take place within the narrative middle.

In *Flóamanna saga*, Þorgils goes to the farm of Björn where he is
told that Björn's father had recently passed away and has returned as
an aftrganga:

> Þat var oft um vetrinn, at Þorgils heyrði lamit úti um
> þekjuna, ok eina nótt var þat, at hann stóð upp, tók öxi í
> hönd sér ok gekk út. Hann sá draug fyrir dyrum standa,
> mikinn ok illiligan. Þorgils færir upp öxina, en þessi snýr
> undan ok til haugsins, ok sem þeir koma þar, snýr drau-
> grinn á móti. Takast þeir fangbrögðum, því at Þorgils
> hafði sleppt öxinni. Var þeira atgangr bæði harðr ok grim-
> miligr, svá at upp gekk jörðin undir fótum þeim. En at
> lyktum varð svá, með því at Þorgilsi var lengra líf ætlat,
> at draugrinn fell á bak aftr, en Þorgils ofan á hann. Tekr
> hann þar þá hvíld ok náir síðan öxi sinni. Höggr Þorgils
> þá af honum höfuð ok mælir síðan yfir honum, at hann
> skuli engum manni at meini verða. Varð ok aldrigi vart
> við hann síðan.[237]

---

[236]Eyrbyggja saga 1935, ch. 63. **Translation:** everyone felt that Lame-foot would not
let up until he had cleared the whole district of both people and livestock, unless a
solution was found (The saga of the people of Eyri 1997, 212.)

[237]Flóamanna saga 1986, ch. 13. **Translation:** Often during the winter Thorgils heard
a lot of thrashing about on the roof. One night he got up, picked up his axe and went
out. He saw a ghost standing in front of the door, huge and hideous-looking. Thorgils
raised his axe, but the ghost ran back to the burial mound and when they got there the
ghost turned on him. They began to wrestle, because Thorgils had dropped the axe.
Their struggle was both grim and fierce and the earth was churned up under their feet.

This narrative could just as easily be about a tröll, and as Ármann Jakobsson reminds us of, it is not always possible to discern the difference.[238] There is nothing distinctly supernatural about this aftrganga, the main difference between it and the trollkona from *Grettis saga* is that it lives in a mound and not in a cave. This aftrganga attacks the farmhouse, i.e. the narrative middle, which is consistent with the hypothesis, but it does neither invoke a sense of wonder nor does it seem unbelievable in the narrative. However, one night Þorgils' friend Auðunn Gyðuson knocks on his door asking for help, as his mother has died and that strange things have been happening since: „Stukku ok allir menn á brottu, því at engir þorðu við at vera. Nú vilda ek fara með hana til greftrar ok fylgdir þú mér."[239] Auðunn explicitly states he wants them to drop the heaviest possible weight on top of the coffin once buried. Horror follows:

> Fara nú síðan, ok sem þeir hafa farit um hríð, tekr at braka
> mjök í kistunni, ok því næst bresta af hankarnir, ok kemst
> Gyða ór kistunni. Þá fara þeir til báðir ok tóku hana, ok
> þurfti þó alls við, ok váru þeir báðir sterkir menn. Þat taka
> þeir til bragða, at þeir flytja hana til báls, er Auðunn hafði
> búit. Síðan kasta þeir henni á bálit ok váru hjá, meðan hon
> brann.[240]

In the end it turned out, because Thorgils was destined to live longer, that the ghost fell onto his back and Thorgils on top of him. He rested a moment and then grabbed his axe. Thorgils cut off his head and then said over him that he would no longer do harm to men; he was never seen again (The Complete Sagas of Icelanders III: 280-1).

[238] Ármann Jakobsson. 2010, 190-192.

[239] Flóamanna saga 1986, ch. 13. **Translation:** All the men have run away, because no one dares remain. I want to go bury her and I want you to come with me (The Complete Sagas of Icelanders III: 281).

[240] Flóamanna saga 1986, ch. 13. **Translation:** Then they started off, and when they had gone a while, there was a lot of creaking in the coffin, and then the ropes broke off

This incident is quite different from the previous one as it involves a great deal of fear, indicating the supernaturality of the events surrounding Gyða's death. She then springs quite unexpectedly from her coffin; the burial and the weight was meant to be precautionary, but she has already attacked them before they can go through with it. Where Björn's father is only borderline supernatural, Gyða is entirely supernatural.

In *Grettis saga*, Glámr returns from the dead and must be dealt with by Grettir Ásmundarson. As Torfi Tulinius points out, just the fact that he is Swedish should arouse suspicion that the supernatural is close by.[241] When he first appears in the saga he his hired to watch over Þórhallr's sheep in the winter. While he is warned that the region is haunted he says that he is not afraid of such things. When he shows up for work he is quickly disliked by the people at the farm. He is "hljóðmikill ok dimmraddaðr, ok féit stǫkk allt saman, þegar hann hóaði. Kirkja var á Þórhallsstǫðum; ekki vildi Glámr til hennar koma; hann var ósǫngvinn ok trúlauss, stirfinn ok viðskotaillr; ǫllum var hann hvimleiðr."[242] Glámr then refuses to fast on Christmas eve, saying that "Marga hindrvitni hafi þér, þá er ek sé til einskis koma; veit ek eigi, at mǫnnum fari nú betr að heldr en þá, er menn fóru ekki með slíkt; þótti mér þá betri siðr, er menn váru heiðnir kallaðir, ok

---

and Gyda got out of the coffin. They both went and grabbed her and it took all they had even though they were both strong men. They decided that they should take her to the pyre which Audun had prepared. Then they threw her onto the pyre and stood nearby while she burned (The Complete Sagas of Icelanders III: 281).

[241] Torfi H. Tulinius. 1999, 294.

[242] **Translation:** He had a deep, booming voice, and the sheep would all flock together when he called out to them. There was a church at Thorhallsstadir, but Glam would not go near it. He was not given to worship and had no faith, but was peevish and rude. Everyone found him obnoxious (The saga of Grettir the strong 1997, 101)

vil ek hafa mat minn, en engar refjur",[243] ignoring when Þórhallr's wife tries to convince him that bad things will befall him if he were to eat on this eve. Sure enough, the worst thing imaginable happens to Glámr:

Veðri var svá farit, at myrkt var um að litask, ok flǫgraði ór drífa, ok gnýmikit, ok versnaði mjǫk sem á leið daginn. Heyrðu menn til sauðamanns ǫndverðan daginn, en miðr er leið á daginn; tók þá at fjúka ok gerði á hríð um kveldit. Kómu menn til tíða, ok leið svá fram at dagsetri. Eigi kom Glámr heim. Var þá um talat, hvárt hans skyldi eigi leita, en fyrir því at hríð var á ok niðamyrkr, þá varð ekki af leitinni. Kom hann eigi heim jólanóttina; biðu menn svá fram um tíðir. At œrnum degi fóru menn í leitina ok fundu féit víða í fǫnnum, lamit af ofviðri eða hlaupit á fjǫll upp. Því næst kómu þeir á traðk mikinn ofarliga í dalnum; þótti þeim því líkt, sem þar hefði glímt verit heldr sterkliga, því at grjótit var víða upp leyst ok svá jǫrðin. Þeir hugðu at vandliga ok sá, hvar glámr lá skammt á brott frá þeim. Hann var dauðr ok blár sem hel, en digr sem naut.[244]

---

[243]**Translation:** You have all sorts of superstitions that I dismiss as worthless. People don't strike me as being any better off now than they were in the days when they didn't practice such things. I preferred the way people were when they were called heathens. I want my food, and don't try any tricks (The saga of Grettir the strong 1997, 101)

[244]**Translation:** It was dark and snow was falling. The weather was stormy and grew much worse as the day progressed. People heard the shepherd early in the day, but less as the day wore on. Then the snow began to drift and in the evening a blizzard got up. Everyone went to mass, and night fell, but Glam did not return home. The idea of going out to look for him was suggested, but because of the raging blizzard and pitch darkness, no search was made. He did not return on Christmas Eve, and everyone waited until the mass was over. When it was fully daylight the people set off to make a search and found sheep scattered among the snowdrifts, thrown around by the storm;

These are the exact same words as are used to describe the dead body of Þórólfr bægifótr in *Eyrbyggja saga*, and the scene implies that Glámr has been killed by a tröll, reminiscent of the tröll Grettir fights later in the saga, and this is indeed the preferred explanation given for his death in the saga as well. Glámr is buried by the church.

> Litlu síðar urðu menn varir við þat, at Glámr lá eigi kyrr.
> Varð mǫnnum at því mikit mein, svá at margir fellu í óvit,
> ef sá hann, en sumir heldu eigi vitinu. Þegar eptir jólin
> þóttusk menn sjá hann heima þar á bœnum. Urðu menn
> ákafliga hræddir; stukku þá margir menn í brott. Því næst
> tók Glámr at ríða húsum á nætr, svá at lá við brotum; gekk
> hann þá náliga nætr ok daga. Varla þorðu menn at fara
> upp í dalinn, þó at ætti nóg ørendi. Þótti mǫnnum þar í
> heraðinu mikit mein at þessu.[245]

This indeed reminds us to a great extent of Þórólfr bægifótr; much af the region becomes derelict as a consequence and people die because of him. When Grettir has come to Þórhallsstaðir and they finally meet,

---

some had fled to the mountains. Then they found a huge trampled area towards the head of the vally, which looked as if a mighty skirmish had taken place there, because rocks and soil had been torn up in many places. They looked more closely and saw Glam lying a short distance way. He was dead, black as hell and bloated to the size of a bull (The saga of Grettir the strong 1997, 101-2.)

[245]Grettis saga Ásmundarsonar 1936, ch. 32 **Translation:** Shortly afterwards, people became aware that Glam was not resting in peace. He wrought such havoc that some people fainted at the sight of him, and others went out of their minds. Immediately after Christmas, people thought they saw him at the farm, and were so terrified that many of them fled. After that, Glam started straddling the roof at night, until it was nearly smashed to pieces. Then his ghost roamed aronud there by day and night. Even people with ample reason for going into the valley hardly dared to venture there. The local people thought this was a terrible plague (The saga of Grettir the strong 1997, 102)

Glámr is described as having a head "afskræmiliga mikit ok undarliga stórskorit".[246]

> Ok í því hljóp Grettir undir hendr honum ok þreif um hann miðjan ok spennti á honum hrygginn sem fastast gat hann, ok ætlaði hann, at Glámr myndi kikna við; en þrællinn lagði at handleggjum Grettis svá fast, at hann horfaði allr fyrir orku sakar [. . .] Vildi Glámr leita út, en Grettir fœrði við fœtr, hvar sem hann mátti, en þó gat Glámr dregit hann fram ór skálanum. Áttu þeir þá allharða sókn, því at þrællinn ætlaði at koma honum út ór bœnum; en svá illt, sem at eiga var við Glám inni, þá sá Grettir, at þó var verra at fásk við hann úti, ok því brauzk hann í móti af ollu afli at fara út. Glámr fœrðisk í aukana ok kneppði hann at sér, er þeir kómu í anddyrit. Ok er Grettir sér, at hann fekk eigi við spornat, hefir hann allt eitt atriðit, at hann hleypr sem harðast í fang þrælnum ok spyrnir báðum fótum í jarðfastan stein, er stóð í durunum. Við þessu bjósk þrællinn eigi; hann hafði þá togazk við at draga Gretti at sér, ok því kiknaði Glámr á bak aptr ok rauk ofugr út á dyrnar, svá at herðarnar námu uppdyrit, ok ræfrit gekk í sundr, bæði viðirnir ok þekjan frørin; fell hann svá opinn ok ofugr út ór húsunum, en Grettir á hann ofan.[247]

---

[246]Grettis saga Ásmundarsonar 1936, ch. 35

[247]**Translation:** At that moment Grettir ducked under Glam's arms and clutched him around the waist, squeezing against his backbone with all his might in the hope of toppling him. But the wretch gripped Grettir's arms so tightly that he was forced to yield his grip [. . .] Glam tried to make it to the door, while Grettir struggled for a foothold. Eventually Glam managed to drag him out of the hall. A mighty fight ensued, because the wretch intended to take him outside the farmhouse. But difficult as Glam

Normally victory would be at hand, but not in the case of Glámr. Even Grettir becomes terrified of him:

Nú í því er Glámr fell, rak skýit frá tunglinu, en Glámr hvessti augun upp í móti, ok svá hefir Grettir sagt sjálfr, at þá eina sýn hafi hann sét svá, at honum brygði við. Þá sigaði svá at honum af ǫllu saman, mœði ok því, er hann sá, at Glámr gaut sínum sjónum harðliga, at hann gat eigi brugðit saxinu ok lá náliga í milli heims ok heljar. En því var meiri ófagnaðarkraptr með Glámi en flestum ǫðrum aptrgǫngumǫnnum, at hann mælti þá á þessa leið[248]

Glámr tells Grettir that he has at this time received half the maturity he would have had he never encountered him, and that from this moment Grettir will never grow stronger, but that his actions will lead to his inevitable exile and death. After telling this to Grettir,

was to deal with indoors, Grettir saw he would be even harder to handle outdoors, so he struggled with all his might to keep him from going out. Glam's strength redoubled and he clutched Grettir towards him when they reached the entrance hall. When Grettir realised that he could not hold him back, in a single move he suddenly thrust himself as hard as he could into the wretch's arms and pressed both feet against a rock that was buried in the grount at the doorway. The wretch was caught unawares, and as he had been straining to pull Grettir towards him, Glam tubmled over backwards and crashed through the door. His shoulders took the door-frame with him and the rafters were torn apart, the wooden roofing and the frozen turf on it, and Glam fell out of the house onto his back, face upwards, with Grettir on top of him (The saga of Grettir the strong 1997, 106.)

[248]**Translation:** Just as Glam fell, the clouds drifted away from the moon and Glam glared up at it. Grettir himself has said that this was the only sight that ever unnerved him. Suddenly Grettir's strength deserted him, from exhaustion and also because of the fierce way Glam was rolling his eyes and, unable to draw his sword, he lay there on the brink of death. Glam was endowed with more evil force than most other ghosts, as he spoke these words (The saga of Grettir the strong 1997, 106-7.)

he regains his concentration, chops off Glámr's head and places it between his buttocks.

Torfi Tulinius points to Glámr's obvious connection with *mirabilium*, but also suggests that perhaps he is of a more demonic nature and would thus rather belong to the *magica*.[249] I am not convinced of that argument however as other Icelandic draugar have everything in common with Glámr and would rather count him as *mirabilia* bordering on the *magica*. He is killed in a horrible fashion for one, which does not seem like the demise of a demon, and demons do not haunt either. His actions resemble that of Þórólfr bægifótr in most ways: he is disliked while living and feared after death. His aversion to church and religion does not necessarily make him demonic, but rather a dislikable, arrogant man who gets his just desserts at the hands of a tröll, as he is warned might happen should he eat on Christmas eve. He possesses superhuman strength and the supernatural ability to curse Grettir. Fear is the most important element associated with Glámr, as he even manages to almost terrify Grettir to death while cursing him. Grettir then removes his head and places it in the appropriate place for the context to keep him from ever returning; his body is then burned to cinders. In all respects, Glámr fits the profile for draugar: he haunts the narrative middle and his supernaturality is unquestionable.

In *Grœnlendinga saga*, Guðríðr sits by her dead husband's corpse who, all of a sudden, sits up and asks where she is:

> Þrjá tíma mælti hann þetta, en hon þagði; þá mælti hon við Þorstein bónda: „Hvárt skal ek svǫr veita hans máli eða eigi?" Hann bað hana eigi svara. Þá gekk Þorsteinn bóndi yfir gólfit ok settisk á stólinn, en Guðríðr sat í knjám honum; ok þá mælti Þorsteinn bóndi: „Hvat villtu nafni?"

---

[249]Torfi H. Tulinius. 1999, 294-5.

segir hann. Hann svarar, er stund leið: „Mér er annt til
þess, at segja Guðríði forlǫg sín, til þess at hon kunni þá
betr andláti mínu, því at ek em kominn til góðra hvíldas-
taða [. . .] ok þá hnígr Þorsteinn aptr, ok var búit um lík
hans ok fœrt til skips.[250]

Þorsteinn returns to a short undead life to let Guðríðr know that he
has received a good afterlife and then tells her fortune before falling
back in peace. This narrative indicates surprise and fear at the talking
corpse and this event takes place in the narrative middle.

There are two encounters with draugar in *Laxdœla saga*. In a minor
one, Guðrún loses her husband Þorkell to drowning, and that same
night she encounters a draugr by the cemetery gate:

> „Mikil tíðendi, Guðrún," sagði hann. Guðrún svarar:
> „Þegi þú yfir þeim þá, armi." Gekk Guðrún til kirkju,
> svá sem hon hafði áðr ætlat, ok er hon kom til kirkjun-
> nar, þá þóttisk hon sjá, at þeir Þorkell váru heim komnir
> ok stóðu úti fyrir kirkju. Hon sá, at sjár rann ór klæðum
> þeira. Guðrún mælti ekki við þá ok gekk inn í kirkju
> og dvalðisk þar slíka hríð, sem henni sýndisk; gengr hon
> síðan inn til stofu, því at hon ætlaði, at þeir Þorkell myndi
> þangat gengnir; ok er hon kom í stofuna, þá var þar ekki

---

[250]Grœnlendinga saga 1935, ch. 5. **Translation:** Three times he spoke these words,
but she remained silent. Then she spoke to Thorstein the farmer: "Shall I answer his
question or not?" He told her not to answer. Thorstein the farmer then crossed the floor
and sat on the chair with Gudrid on his knee. Then Thorstein the farmer spoke: "What
is it you want, namesake?" he said. He answered after a short pause: "I want to tell
Gudrid her fate, to make it easier for her to resign herself to my death, for I have gone
to a good resting place [. . .] At that Thorstein fell back and his corpse was made ready
and taken to the ship (The saga of the Greenlanders 1997, 27.)

manna. Þá brá Guðrúnu mjǫk í brún um atburð þenna
allan jafnsaman.[251]

These draugar are all encountered in the narrative middle and though
Guðrún courageously replies to the first one's sneers, she is shaken
by this whole event.

The other draugr in *Laxdæla saga* is Hrappr, who before he dies
requests of his wife Vigdís that she to bury him standing up inside
the walls of the main hall, a request not to be followed through on for
the value of human life. She does it anyway and in fact it is implied
in the text that she did not dare do anything else out of fear (svá at
hon treystisk eigi ǫðru), and therefore it is implied that the haunting
is inevitable whether or not Vigdís does as Hrappr demands.

> En svá illr sem hann var viðreignar, þá er hann lifði, þá
> jók nú miklu við, er hann var dauðr, því at hann gekk
> mjǫk aptr. Svá segja menn, at hann deyddi flest hjón sín í
> aptrgǫngunni; hann gerði mikinn ómaka þeim flestum er
> í nánd bjuggu; var eyddr bœrinn á Hrappsstǫðum.[252]

---

[251] Laxdœla saga 1934, ch. 76. **Translation:** "News of great moment, Gudrun," it said,
and Gudrun answered, "Then keep silent about it, you wretch." Gudrun went towards
the church as she had intended and when she had reached the church she thought
she saw that Thorkel and his companions had arrived home and stood outside of the
church. She saw the seawater dripping from their clothing. Gudrun did not speak to
them but entered the church and stayed there as long as she cared to. She then returned
to the main room, thinking that Thorkel and his companions would have gone there.
When she reached the house there was no one there. Gudrun was then very shaken by
all these occurrences (The saga of the people of Laxardal 1997, 117)

[252] **Translation:** But if it had been difficult to deal with him when he was alive, he was
much worse dead, for he haunted the area relentlessly. It is said that in his haunting
he killed most of his servants. To most of the people living in the vicinity he caused no
end of difficulty and the farm at Hrappsstadir became deserted (The saga of the people
of Laxardal 1997, 19.)

Even his widow Vigdís leaves the derelict farmstead at Hrappsstaðir.[253]
His body is then removed and Hrappr's haunting is to a great degree
diminished. His son Sumarliði moves in afterwards, but becomes de-
ranged and dies shortly thereafter. Later, the farm is bought by Óláfr
Hǫskuldsson and Hrappr comes yet again to terrorize the farmstead.

> Húskarl gengr at fjósdurunum. Óláfr finnr eigi, fyrr en
> hann hleypr í fang honum; spyrr Óláfr, hví hann fœri svá
> fæltiliga. Hann svarar: „Hrappr stendr í fjósdurunum ok
> vildi fálma til mín, en ek em saddr á fangbrǫgðum við
> hann."[254]

Óláfr then digs up the body and deals with it in the same manner
that Þórólfr bægifótr was dealt with, by burning it. "Heðan frá verðr
engum manni mein at aptrgǫngu Hrapps."[255] The same applies to
Hrappr as the other draugar mentioned so far: he invokes fear, he
kills people and obliterates whole regions. He also obeys the principle
suggested by the hypothesis by remaining in the narrative middle.

The only draugr in *Brennu-Njáls saga* is a completely different one
from the rest in that he never leaves the liminal space yet he appears
before his living friends and family. It is the scene of Gunnarr á
Hlíðarenda singing in his mound, which was mentioned earlier in
this paper.

---

[253]Laxdœla saga 1934, ch. 17.

[254]Laxdœla saga 1934, ch. 24. **Translation:** The servant went toward the door of the
cowshed but suddenly came running back into Olaf's arms. When Olaf asked what
had frightened him so the servant answered, Hrapp is standing there in the doorway,
reaching out for me, and I've had my fill of wrestling with him" (The saga of the people
of Laxardal 1997, 35)

[255]**Translation:** No one else was harmed by Hrappr's haunting after that (The saga of
the people of Laxardal 1997, 35)

Sá atburðr varð at Hlíðarenda, at smalamaðr ok griðkona
ráku fé hjá haugi Gunnars; þeim þótti Gunnarr vera kátr ok
kveða í hauginum. Fóru þau heim ok sǫgðu Rannveigu,
móður Gunnars, atburðinn, en hon bað þau segja Njáli;
þau fóru til Bergþórshváls ok sǫgðu Njáli, en hann lét þau
segja sér þrim sinnum.[256]

Skarpheðinn and Gunnar's son Hǫgni are later out walking south of
Gunnar's mound one evening when they notice that the mound has
been opened:

ok hafði Gunnarr snúizk í hauginum ok sá í móti tunglinu;
þeir þóttusk fjǫgur ljós sjá brenna í hauginum, ok bar
hvergi skugga á. Þeir sá, at Gunnarr var kátligr ok með
gleðimóti miklu. Hann kvað vísu ok svá hátt, at þó mátti
heyra gǫrla, þó at þeir væri firr [...] Síðan lauksk aptr
haugrinn.[257]

They realize that no one will ever believe this has taken place, but
take this as a challenge from Gunnarr and decide to avenge him.
The boundary between the saga world and the otherworld is never
broken; it appears that what Skarpheðinn and Hǫgni see is not in their

---

[256]Brennu-Njáls saga 1954, ch. 78. **Translation:** One day at Hlidarendi it happened
that a shepherd and a servant woman were driving cattle past Gunnar's mound. Gunnar seemed to them to be in high spirits and reciting verses in the mound They went
home and told Gunnar's mother Rannveig about this, and she asked them to tell Njal.
They went off to Bergthorshvol and told him, and he had them repeat it three times
(The Complete Sagas of Icelanders III: 91).

[257]Brennu-Njáls saga 1954, ch. 79. **Translation:** Gunnar had turned around to look at
the moon. They thought that they saw four lights burning in the mound, and that there
were no shadows. They saw that Gunnar was happy and had a very cheerful look. He
recited a verse so loudly that they could hear it clearly, even at a distance [...] Then
the mound closed again (The Complete Sagas of Icelanders III: 91).

world, but that they catch a glimpse into the otherworld from where they are standing in the mortal realm. This event is unbelievable to all but those who see it for themselves, yet this account diverges from the others in that Gunnarr never crosses the boundary and is therefore not encountered as such; the border between the worlds is neither crossed by him nor Skarpheðinn or Hǫgni.

In *Færeyinga saga* we only get a vague description, while still retaining the foreboding of imminent threat:

> "Ok er á leið haustit fundust rekar af skipi þeirra í Austrey,
> ok er vetr kom, gerðust afturgöngur miklar í Götu ok víða í
> Austrey, ok sýndust þeir oft frændr Þrándar, ok varð mön-
> num at þessu mikit mein. Sumir fengu beinbrot eðr önnur
> meiðsl. Þeir sóttu Þránd svá mjök, at hann þorði hvergi
> einn at ganga um vetrinn. Var nú mikit orð á þessu."[258]

These afturgöngur, like most, retain to the narrative middle and are feared.

In chapter 36 of *Vatnsdœla saga*, it is simply said that after the magical (fjölkunnug) Gróa causes a mudslide close to Hof in Hrútafjörður where she lives, and is driven off, "þótti reimt jafnan síðan, er byggð Gró hafði verit, ok vildu menn þar eigi búa frá því upp."[259] This is the

---

[258]Færeyinga saga 1945, 348. This chapter is only preserved in Flateyjarbók, written shortly before 1387 (Færeyinga saga. Ólafur Halldórsson bjó til prentunar: 124). **My translation:** And when the fall went by, remains of their ship was found in Austrey. And when winter came, there was much haunting (afturgöngur can refer both to the haunting and the draugar themselves) in Gata and in many places in Austrey, and Þrándr's friends revealed themselves often and many people suffered by this. Some of them had their bones broken or received other injuries. They seeked Þrándr with such intensity that he did not dare walk by himself in any place during the winter. There was much talk of this.

[259]Vatnsdœla saga 1939, ch. 36. Translation: Ever afterwards the place where Groa

same fear of hauntings as is evident in *Eyrbyggja saga*, *Grettis saga* and other sagas.

We have a more interesting example in *Svarfdæla saga*. The rather unpleasant Klaufi comes home to his wife Yngvildr, who deceives him:

> Hon dvaldi fyrir Klaufa, þar til at hann var laginn í gegnum, svá hann fekk þegar bana. Þessu verki ollu þeir Ásgeirssynir, ok tóku þeir Klaufa ok drógu undir heygarð at húsabaki. Yngvildr fór þá í rekkju sína, en þeir bjuggust á brott. Þegar kom Klaufi til sængr Yngvildar, er þeir váru á brott farnir. Hon lét þá kalla á þá bræðr, ok hjuggu þeir af honum höfuðit ok lögðu neðan við iljarnar.[260]

Klaufi is very persistent to say the least. When his head has been cut off he alerts his kinsmen to his murder by reciting a verse:

> Sitk á húsi.
> Sék til þess:
> Heðan munum vér
> oss hefnda vænta.[261]

---

lived seemed haunted, and men had no wish to live there from that time on (The saga of the people of Vatnsdal 1997, 48)

[260]Svarfdæla saga 1986, ch. 22 (ch. 19 in some versions, ch. 17 in translation) **Translation:** She delayed Klaufi until he had been run through with the sword, and he died on the spot. Yngvild's brothers performed this deed, and they took Klaufi and dragged him under a haystack behind the house. Yngvild went to bed, and they prepared to leave. But in the moment that they left, Klaufi got into bed with Yngvild. She had her brothers called back, and they cut off his head and laid it down by his feed (The Complete Sagas of Icelanders IV: 173)

[261]**My translation:** I sit on the house / I will see to it / that from this moment / we expect revenge (secondary translation in The Complete Sagas of Icelanders IV: 174: I sit on the house, / hopeful of revenge, / hence will all of us / welcome the revenge).

Karl inn rauði hears this and notices that:

> „Alllíkt er þetta rómi Klaufs, frænda várs, þá er vér heyrðum
> til hans, ok má vera hann þykkist nökkurs við þurfa. Fellr
> mér svá í hug kveðskapr sjá, at víst er þetta fyrir stórtíðen-
> dum, hvárt sem þau eru fram komin eða eigi." Ok fara
> þeir út eftir þetta alvápnaðir ok ætla at snúa yfir til Hofs.
> Þá sá þeir ekki lítinn grepp suðr við garðinn, ok var þat
> Klaufi ok hafði höfuðit í hendi sér ok mælti:

> Suðr es ok suðr es
> Svá skulum stefna.[262]

In this fashion, Klaufi leads his kinsmen to the house of his killers, but
they are ready for them and a big battle ensues. Then Klaufi interferes
with the battle:

> Þá kom Klaufi í bardaga ok barði blóðgu höfðinu á báðar
> hendr bæði hart ok tíðum, ok þá kom flótti í lið Ljótólfs.
> Því var líkast sem þá er melrakki kemr í sauðadun. Þeir
> Ljótólfr heldu nú undan, ok eru nú níu eftir, en fimmtán
> heldu til, en sjau váru hinir, ok ætlar Ljótólfr at snúa ofan
> Bleikudal fyrir ofan Bakkagarð. En þar var Klaufi fyrir ok
> bannaði þeim þar at fara. Út snúa þeir undan ok ætla
> ofan Nafarsdal fyrir útan teiginn. Eigi var þess kostr,

---

[262]**Translation:** "The voice is very much like the one that our kinsman Klaufi had
when we used to hear him, and it can be that he has something important in mind.
It occurs to me that this poem signifies some great event, whether it has happened or
will soon do so". Afterwards they went out fully armed intending to go over to Hof.
Then they saw a strange being, by no means little, south of the hayfield, and it was
Klaufi, holding his head in his hand. He spoke: Southwards, to the south, / surely we
are bound (The Complete Sagas of Icelanders IV: 174).

Klaufi var þar fyrir. Þá bar Karl at ok tókst bardagi í
annat sinn. Undan varð Ljótólfr at halda, er þeir höfðu
skamma stund barizt, því at Klaufi var þá í bardaganum.
Sjau váru þeir Ljótólfr, er þeir heldu undan, en hinir fjórir.
Allt fór Ljótólfr, til þess er hann kom heim at garðinum at
Hofi. Eigi var þá kostr at fara lengra eða í hliðit, því at
Klaufi var þar fyrir. Þá bar Karl at, ok urðu þeir at berjast
í þriðja sinn, þegar er þeim laust saman.[263]

No matter how they try, they cannot escape the wrath of Klaufi, who
is largely in control of the battle. Ljótólfr and his men panic and try
crying out so that their friend Skíði can come to their aid and join
the fight. He hears their call and manages to get Ljótólfr and his last
companion indoors before they would have been killed.

This is the one incident of two in Íslendingasögur where draugar
take part in a battle. The precautions taken with Klaufi's body are not
adequate; they forget to place his head between his buttocks for one.
Klaufi then returns and wreaks havoc, pummeling his foes with his
own severed head. His kinsmen do not fear him as it is clear from

---

[263]Svarfdæla saga 1986, ch. 23 **Translation:** Then Klaufi waded into the battle, wildly
swinging his bloody head back and forth on both sides until Ljotolf's troops began to
scatter. It was as if a fox were loose in a flock of sheep. Ljotolf and his troops retreated
until only nine of his original fifteen were facing seven of the enemy. Ljotolf intended
to turn down into Bleikudal just beside Bakkagard, but Klaufi blocked their path. Then
they tried to go the other way down into Nafarsdal just outside the paddock, but this
was no better, for Klaufi was there also. Then Karl came at them, and the battle began
again. Ljotolf was forced to retreat after they had fought for a while because Klaufi was
in the battle. Ljotolf's force was now seven, which further retreated, and the enemy
four. Ljotolf did not stop until he came to the hayfield wall at Hof, but it was not
possible to enter through the gate because Klaufi was blocking it. Then Karl came at
them, and they were forced to do battle a third time (The Complete Sagas of Icelanders
IV: 176).

the onset that Klaufi needs help to avenge his murder. Even though it seems that he cannot do this alone, he can help once the battle has started. The narrative suggests that Klaufi does not actually kill anyone himself, and the most likely explanation is that he is unable to. What he does is terrify his enemies while his kinsmen fight, not only by carrying his head for the added effect, but simply by being there against the laws of nature. This account indicates that this encounter is extremely supernatural, and it happens in the narrative middle of the saga.

The second incident of battling draugar is in Bárðar saga Snæfellsáss, which has been previously mentioned apropos Ármann Jakobsson 2006. Gestr Bárðarson is sent to collect the treasures buried with king Raknarr. Of him it is said that: "Hefir hann ráðit fyrir Hellulandi ok mörgum öðrum löndum. Ok er hann hafði lengi löndum ráðit, lét hann kviksetja sig með fimm hundruð manna á Raknaslóða. Hann myrði föður sinn ok móður ok margt annat fólk."[264] Gestr and his companions sail to the Greenland and from there on to Helluland.[265] There on the narrative periphery they find king Raknarr's mound. It proves difficult to gain entry as when they have opened the mound in the evening, it is always closed again the morning after, so the priest decides to wake in the opening during the following night. There he witnesses the most amazing things:

> Ok er á leið at miðri nótt, sá hann Raknar, ok var hann
> fagrbúinn. Hann bað prest fara með sér ok kveðst góða

---

[264] Bárðar saga Snæfellsáss 1986, ch. 18.

[265] This land is also mentioned in Grœnlendinga saga 1935, and Eiríks saga rauða. It may be mentioned on the side that Gestr encounters an aggressive bull there which he is unable to defend himself from, until Jósteinn the priest hits its spine with a crucifix, at which the bull disappears into the earth never to be seen again (Bárðar saga Snæfellsáss, ch. 18). This bull is obviously a manifestation of the Devil.

skyldu hans ferð gera, – „ok er hér hringr, er ek vil gefa
þér, ok men." Engu svarar prestr ok sat kyrr sem áðr.
Mörg fádæmi sýndust honum, bæði tröll ok óvættir, fjandr
ok fjölkunnigar þjóðir. Sumir blíðkuðu hann, en sumir
ógnuðu honum, at hann skyldi þá heldr burtu ganga en
áðr. Þar þóttist hann sjá frændr sína ok vini, jafnvel Óláf
konung með hirð sinni, ok bað hann með sér fara. Sá hann
ok, at Gestr ok hans félagar bjuggust ok ætluðu í burt ok
kölluðu, at Jósteinn prestr skyldi fylgja þeim ok flýta sér í
burt. Ekki gaf prestr um þetta, ok hvat undrum sem hann
sá eða hversu ólmliga þessir fjandr létu, þá kómu þeir þó
aldri nær presti sakir vatns þess, er hann stökkti. Í móti
degi hurfu þessi undr öll af. Kom Gestr þá ok hans menn
til haugsins. Ekki sá þeir presti brugðit um nökkut.[266]

This event indicates that there may be some devilry about rather than
your everyday draugar. This is further confirmed once Gestr spelunks
into the mound and sees the ship they were buried with which was
not possible to commandeer with fewer than five hundred men.

Þar sá hann Raknar sitja á stóli. Furðu var hann ílliligr
at sjá. Bæði var þar fúlt ok kalt. Kistill stóð undir fótum hans fullr af fé. Men hafði hann á hálsi sér harðla
glæsiligt ok digran gullhring á hendi. Í brynju var hann
ok hafði hjálm á höfði ok sverð í hendi. Gestr gekk at
Raknari, en kvaddi hann virðuligri konungskveðju, en
Raknarr hneigði honum á móti [...] Raknarr veik þá
at honum höfðinu með hjálminum. Tók Gestr hann, ok
því næst færði Gestr hann ór brynjunni, ok var Raknarr

<hr>

[266] Bárðar saga Snæfellsáss 1986, ch. 19.

hinn auðveldasti. Alla gripina hafði hann af Raknari nema
sverðit, því at þá er Gestr tók til þess, spratt Raknarr upp
ok rann á Gest. Hvárki fann þá á honum, at hann væri
gamall né stirðr. Þá var ok albrunnit kertit konungsnautr.
Trylldist Raknarr svá, at Gestr varð allr forviða fyrir. Þóttist Gestr þá sjá vísan dauða sinn. Upp stóðu ok allir þeir,
sem í skipinu váru.[267]

As has previously been explored, Gestr calls out for his father Bárðr
Snæfellsáss to come to his aid, but the dead confuse him so that he
cannot help Gestr. He then turns to St. Óláfr Tryggvason:

Eftir þat sá Gestr Óláf konung koma í hauginn með ljósi
miklu. Við þá sýn brá Raknari svá, at ór honum dró afl
allt. Þá gekk Gestr svá fast at, at Raknarr fell á bak aftr
með tilstilli Óláfs konungs. Þá hjó Gestr höfuð af Raknari
ok lagði þat við þjó honum. Allir inir dauðu settust niðr
við kvámu Óláfs konungs, hverr í sitt rúm.[268]

This scene is reminiscent of the many scenes in Fornaldarsögur Helen
F. Leslie and Rosemary Powers examine in their respective articles on
journeys to the otherworld. Daniel Sävborg has argued in contrast
to the celebrated opinion that *Bárðar saga* as a post-classical Íslendingasaga borrows heavily from the Fornaldarsögur, but rather that it is
synonymous with both younger and earlier folk legends:

On the other hand, these peculiarities are not present in
most episodes about encounters with the Otherworld of
fornaldarsögur or riddarasögur. There, on the contrary,

---

[267] Bárðar saga Snæfellsáss 1986, ch. 20.
[268] Bárðar saga Snæfellsáss 1986, ch. 20.

we have many of the characteristics of the folktale. This recalls my earlier conclusion that the episodes in Bergbúa þáttr and Bárðar saga discussed above can be described as legends, and this in basically the same sense as the legends that are recorded during the 19th and 20th centuries. Another of the differences is that the legend was regarded as fundamentally true, while the folktale was not perceived as true but as pure 'entertainment', that is: not as history. This does not at all mean that it really was true, but that it was told with that claim and appears to have been perceived as such by its intended audience.[269]

This view that the veracity of the tale did not suffer for its more legendary traits is shared by Ármann Jakobsson (1998) and myself. In this light, *Bárðar saga* does not deviate as radically from other Íslendingasögur. The main difference is that of the draugar's relation to the narrative middle.

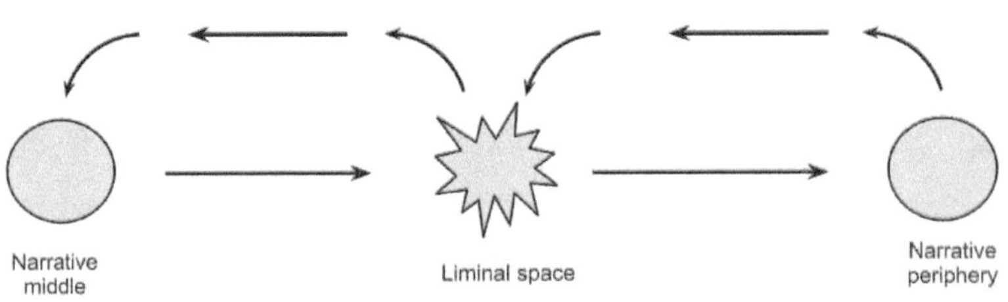

If we again look at the rules of the travel narrative, Gestr first travels to Greenland (narrative middle > liminal space > narrative middle).

---

[269]Sävborg, Daniel. 2012,

Thence he travels to Helluland (narrative middle > liminal space > narrative periphery), and in Helluland Gestr enters the mound (narrative periphery > liminal space). Thus the draugar are met far outside the narrative middle of the saga and in this respect they are the only draugar in the whole corpus of Íslendingasögur who break this rule; they are not afturgöngur in the sense that they do not return to the realm of the living, but keep to their grave, unlike the other draugar in Íslendingasögur who stalk the living at home. Raknarr and his five hundred fellow interred are in all ways supernatural as the other draugar, but they are closer to being *magica* than *mirabilia*, as they use *sjónhverfingar* (illusions) which are only attributed to devils, and that they are kept at bay by a Christian saint while the protagonist chops off Raknarr's head, whereas his father the pagan semi-saint cannot help. The other draugar then go to rest.

4. Conclusion

In this paper I have argued for a general distinction of uncanny beings made in the diagram presented in the first chapter (*figure 1*, p. 13), excluding the fantastic altogether as the term 'fantastic' does not fit into the world view of the Íslendingasögur.[270] Other supernatural phenomena such as witchcraft was excluded from this paper for reasons of brevity and that magical capabilities neither preclude humans nor said beings. I will especially look further into witchcraft in the future.

The fact that all medieval sagas are essentially Christian literature must be kept in mind. As is shown in chapter 2, folk belief in various ófreskjur was incorporated into the medieval Christian world view as this belief was very real and had to be dealt with; from this root spring the medieval bestiaries and the allegorical meanings behind their various monsters. These creatures only lived on the peripheries of the civilized world. This same applies to finngálkn and flugdrekar in Íslendingasögur and they too are easily explicable within the natural realm of the sagas. They are not by any means supernatural or fantastic. Within the Christian world view we also find a fear of the living dead for they do not belong to God's Creation; they are an inexplicable abomination, and this to somewhat a similar degree applies to tröll.

The narrative model of the supernatural (*figure 1*) hypothesizes only three factors, each with a number of subfactors, for encounters with three types of beings: 1) the place in which an encounter with an ófreskja, tröll or draugur occurs (the narrative middle, a liminal space, the narrative periphery); 2) how natural, borderline natural or

---

[270]More extensively illustrated in Arngrímur Vídalín 2012.

supernatural this occurrence is perceived to be within the narrative (fear and wonder is a clear indication of supernatural phenomena); 3) the proximity to the narrative middle, where supernatural occurrences are hypothesized to take place, a figurative liminal space, or the narrative periphery, where monstrous beings are hypothesized to be found, should be consistent with the supernaturality of the occurrence and which kind of creature is encountered. Of the beings analyzed in this paper, twenty out of twenty five encounters follow the general rule stated in the hypothesis, only two of which break both the rules of relation to the narrative middle and of their supernaturality.

The narrative model is a simple construct which yields complicated results; it is a tool to analyse literature based on a set of ground rules which was not obvious whether the literature adhered to. This should not be understood in such a way that I believe that this is the only way of viewing the supernatural in Íslendingasögur, or that no further analysis is needed. Literature is more complicated than that. The narrative model is meant for surface research only, and yet it predicted results with great accuracy which may be used to found upon more intensive research of supernatura in all genres of medieval Icelandic literature in the future.

For its intents and purposes the hypothesis can be considered accurate and the main conclusions are:

- There is a sense of 'otherness' present in travel narratives from ancient to modern times. The self cannot exist without the other.

- This seems to be equally true in the case of visionary travels and pilgrimages. Travels were important both from a material and a spiritual point of view. Imbued in the world view was a theological, allegorical meaning of a heavenly world order and a holy code of moral. The 'other' in this context is the godless, he who strays from the path of God; the 'self' being the pious, selfless Christian.

- The monstrous, a definite other, was an integral part of this world view, depicted on world maps as being a factual part of the divine order by various theological authorities, and described in travelogues and other contemporary narratives as strange and undesirable races, stories of whom gained immense popular interest.

- In an attempt to reconcile the existence of these monstrous beings, they were adopted into Christian canon by no lesser prophets than Isidore of Seville and St. Augustine. In every respect, the monstrous thus undoubtedly belonged to the medieval Christian world view.

- This understanding of the monstrous is also evident in medieval Icelandic literature.

- The farther the protagonist travels from the narrative middle, the more likely it is that he will come across a) tröll, when a liminal space is reached, and b) ófreskjur, when the periphery is reached. Conversely, he is more likely to encounter draugar the closer he is to the narrative middle.

- The farther the protagonist travels from the narrative middle, the less likely it is that he meets supernatural beings. Conversely, the closer he is to the narrative middle, the more likely it is that he witnesses supernatural occurences and/or beings.

- Draugar are in all ways supernatural and ófreskjur are in all ways natural, while tröll rock the balance between the two.

148

- This narrative function has its roots in contemporary Christian culture.

References

Alighieri, D. (2010). *Gleðileikurinn guðdómlegi*. Reykjavík: Mál og menning.

Ármann Jakobsson. (1998). History of the trolls? bárðar saga as an historical narrative. Printed in *Saga Book*, Volume 25. London: Viking society for Northern Research – University College London.

Ármann Jakobsson. (2006). The good, the bad and the ugly: Bárðar saga and its giants. Printed in *The fantastic in Old Norse/Icelandic literature. Sagas and the British isles: preprint papers of the 13th International Saga Conference Durham and York, 6th-12th August, 2006*. Durham: The Centre for Medieval and Renaissance Studies, Durham University.

Ármann Jakobsson. (2008a). Hvað er tröll? Printed in *Galdramenn. Galdrar og samfélag á miðöldum: Greinar frá ráðstefnu Vestfjarða á miðöldum, Laugarbóli 1. og 2. september 2006*. Reykjavík: Hugvísindastofnun Háskóla Íslands.

Ármann Jakobsson. (2008b). Hversu argur er óðinn? seiður, kynferði og hvamm-sturla. Printed in *Galdramenn. Galdrar og sam-*

félag á miðöldum: Greinar frá ráðstefnu Vestfjarða á miðöldum, Lau-garbóli 1. og 2. september 2006. Reykjavík: Hugvísindastofnun Háskóla Íslands.

Ármann Jakobsson. (2008c). The trollish acts of Þorgrímr the witch. the meanings of troll and ergi in medieval iceland. Printed in *Saga book vol. 32.* London: Viking society for Northern Research – University College London.

Ármann Jakobsson. (2009a). The fearless vampire killers: a note about the icelandic draugr and demonic contamination in grettis saga. Printed in *Folklore vol. 120.* London: Folklore Society.

Ármann Jakobsson. (2009b). Identifying the ogre: The legendary saga giants. Printed in Agneta Ney, Ármann Jakobsson, Annette Lassen (Ed.), *Fornaldarsagaerne: Myter og virkelighed.* København: Museum Tusculanums Forlag - Københavns Universitet.

Ármann Jakobsson. (2010). Íslenskir draugar frá landnámi til lúter-strúar: Inngangur að draugafræðum. Printed in *Skírnir 184 (vor).* Reykjavík: Hið íslenska bókmenntafélag.

Arngrímur Vídalín (2012). Að mæla róteindir með gráðuboga: um fantasíuhugtakið í miðaldabókmenntum. Forthcoming.

Árni Magnússon (1962). *Galdramálin í Thisted.* Reykjavík: Almenna bókafélagið.

Árni Sigurjónsson. (1991). *Bókmenntakenningar fyrri alda.* Reykjavík: Heimskringla - háskólaforlag Máls og menningar.

Ásgeir Blöndal Magnússon. (1989). *Íslensk orðsifjabók.* Reykjavík: Orðabók Háskólans.

Baetke, W. (1950). *Die Götterlehre der Snorra-Edda.* Weimar: Hermann Böhlaus Nachfolger.

Bagge, Sverre. (2009). Nordic uniqueness in the middle ages? political and literary aspects. Printed in *Gripla XX*. Reykjavík: Stofnun Árna Magnússonar á Íslandi.

Bard's saga (1997). Translated by Sarah M. Anderson. Printed in *The Complete Sagas of Icelanders II*. Reykjavík: Leifur Eiríksson Publishing.

Bárðar saga Snæfellsáss (1986). Íslendinga sögur III. Reykjavík: Íslendingasagnaútgáfan.

Beck, H. (1993). Gylfaginning und theologie. Printed in *Snorri Sturluson. ScriptOralia*, Volume 51. Tübingen: Gunter Narr Verlag.

Bergbúa þáttr (1986). Íslendinga sögur IV. Reykjavík: Íslendingasagnaútgáfan.

Bjarnar saga Hítdœlakappa (1938). Íslenzk fornrit III. Reykjavík: Íslenzka fornritaútgáfan.

Boulhosa, Patricia Pires. (2005). *Icelanders and the Kings of Norway. Mediaeval Sagas and Legal Texts*. Leiden - Boston: Brill.

Brennu-Njáls saga (1954). Volume XII of *Íslenzk fornrit*. Reykjavík: Hið íslenzka fornritafélag.

Butler, J. (1993). *Bodies that Matter*.

Clunies Ross, Margaret (1987). *Skáldskaparmál: Snorri Sturluson's ars poetica and medieval theories of language*. Number 4 in Viking Collection. Odense: Odense University Press.

Cormack, Margaret. (1992). "fjǫlkunnigri kono scallatu í faðmi sofa": Sex and the supernatural in icelandic saints' lives. Printed in *Skáldskaparmál 2*. Reykjavík: Stafaholt hf.

Cormack, Margaret. (1994). Visions, demons and gender in the sagas of icelandic saints. Printed in *Collegium Medievale 2*.

Dinzelbacher, Peter. (2005). Die mittelalterliche allegorie der lebensreise. Printed in Leif Søndergaard, Rasmus Thorning Hansen (Ed.), *Monsters, Marvels and Miracles: Imaginary Journeys and Landscapes in the Middle Ages*. University Press of Southern Denmark.

Dronke, Ursula and Peter (1977). The prologue of the prose edda. explorations of a latin background. Printed in *Sjötíu ritgerðir helgaðar Jakobi Benediktssyni 20. júlí 1977*. Reykjavík: Stofnun Árna Magnússonar á Íslandi.

Eddukvæði (1998). Reykjavík: Mál og menning.

Edson, Evelyn. (2005). Mapping the middle ages. Printed in *Monsters, Marvels and Miracles: Imaginary Journeys and Landscapes in the Middle Ages*. Odense: University Press of Southern Denmark.

Egil's saga (1997). Translated by Bernard Scudder. Printed in *The Complete Sagas of Icelanders I*. Reykjavík: Leifur Eiríksson Publishing.

Egils saga Skalla-Grímssonar (1933). Íslenzk fornrit II. Reykjavík: Hið íslenzka fornritafélag.

Einar Ól. Sveinsson. (1954). Íslenzk fornrit xiii. Printed in *Brennu-Njáls saga*. Reykjavík: Hið íslenzka fornritafélag.

Elucidarius (1989). Printed in *Þrjár þýðingar lærðar frá miðöldum. Elucidarius, Um kostu og löstu, Um festarfé sálarinnar*. Reykjavík: Hið íslenska bókmenntafélag.

Eyrbyggja saga (1935). Íslenzk fornrit IV. Reykjavík: Hið íslenzka fornritafélag.

Færeyinga saga (1944-1945). Printed in *Flateyjarbók I & II*, pp. I. 132–164, 403–10; II. 33–42, 340–350, 512–522. Akranes: Flateyjarútgáfan.

Faulkes, A. (1993). The sources of skáldskaparmál: Snorri's intellectual background. Printed in *Snorri Sturluson. ScriptOralia*, Volume 51. Tübingen: Gunter Narr Verlag.

Finnboga saga ramma (1986). Íslendinga sögur IX. Reykjavík: Íslendingasagnaútgáfan.

Fljótsdæla saga (1950). Íslenzk fornrit XI. Reykjavík: Hið íslenzka fornritafélag.

Flóamanna saga (1986). Íslendinga sögur XII. Reykjavík: Íslendingasagnaútgáfan.

Friedman, John Block. (2005). Monsters at the earth's imagined corners. Printed in *Monsters, Marvels and Miracles: Imaginary Journeys and Landscapes in the Middle Ages*. Odense: University Press of Southern Denmark.

Gesta Danorum (2000). *(Saxo's Danmarks Historie). 1. bind*. Gad (Nørhaven, Viborg): Det Danske Sprog- og Litteraturselskab.

Gísla saga Súrssonar (1943). Volume VI of *Íslenzk fornrit*. Reykjavík: Hið íslenzka fornritafélag.

Gísli Sigurðsson. (2002). *Túlkun Íslendingasagna í ljósi munnlegrar hefðar. Tilgáta um aðferð*. Reykjavík: Stofnun Árna Magnússonar á Íslandi.

Gísli Sigurðsson. (2009). Þögnin um gelísk áhrif á íslandi. Printed in *Greppaminni. Rit til heiðurs Vésteini Ólasyni sjötugum*. Reykjavík: Hið íslenska bókmenntafélag.

Gisli Sursson's saga (1997). Translated by Martin S. Regal. Printed in *The Complete Sagas of Icelanders II*. Reykjavík: Leifur Eiríksson Publishing.

Gold-Thorir's saga (1997). Translated by Anthony Maxwell. Printed in *The Complete Sagas of Icelanders III*. Reykjavík: Leifur Eiríksson Publishing.

Grágás (1992). Reykjavík: Mál og menning.

Grettis saga Ásmundarsonar (1936). Íslenzk fornrit VII. Reykjavík: Hið íslenzka fornritafélag.

Grœnlendinga saga (1935). Íslenzk fornrit IV. Reykjavík: Hið íslenzka fornritafélag.

Grundmann, H. (1958). Litteratus-illiteratus. die wandlung einer bildungsnorm vom altertum zum mittelalter. Printed in *Archiv für Kulturgeschichte*, Volume 40.

Gunnar Harðarson. (1989). Inngangur. Printed in *Þrjár þýðingar lærðar frá miðöldum. Elucidarius, Um kostu og löstu, Um festarfé sálarinnar*. Reykjavík: Hið íslenska bókmenntafélag.

Gunnell, Terry (2002). Komi þeir sem koma vilja ... sagnir um innrás óvætta á jólum til forna á íslenska sveitabæi. Printed in Baldur Hafstað og Haraldur Bessason (Ed.), *Úr manna minnum*. Reykjavík: Heimskringla - háskólaforlag Máls og menningar.

Gurevich, Aron. (1988). *Medieval Popular Culture. Problems of belief and perception*. New York, New Rochelle, Melbourne, Sydney: Cambridge University Press.

Guðmundar saga biskups (1953). Byskupa sögur II. Reykjavík: Íslendingasagnaútgáfan.

Hallgerður Hallgrímsdóttir. (2005). *Please yoursELF: Sex With the Icelandic Invisibles*. Reykjavík.

Hastrup, K. (1985). *Culture and History in Medieval Iceland. An anthropological analysis of structure and change*. Oxford: Clarendon Press.

Hastrup, Kirsten. (2009). Northern barbarians: Icelandic canons of civilization. Printed in *Gripla XX*. Reykjavík: Stofnun Árna Magnússonar á Íslandi.

Helga Kress (2006). Grey þykir mér freyja. Printed in *Konur og kristsmenn. Þættir úr kristnisögu Íslands*. Reykjavík: Háskólaútgáfan.

Helgi Guðmundsson. (2003). Þorláks saga biskups og isidor. Printed in *Gripla XIV*. Reykjavík: Stofnun Árna Magnússonar á Íslandi.

Heslop, Kate. (2008). Hearing voices: Uncanny moments in the íslendingasögur. Printed in *Gripla XIX*. Reykjavík: Stofnun Árna Magnússonar á Íslandi.

Hreinn Benediktsson. (1972). *The First Grammatical Treatise*. Reykjavík: Institute of Nordic Linguistics.

Jón Árnason. (2003). *Íslenskar þjóðsögur og ævintýri*. Reykjavík: Bókaútgáfan Þjóðsaga.

Jón Hnefill Aðalsteinsson. (1988). Þjóðtrú. Printed in *Íslensk þjóðmenning V. Trúarhættir: Norræn trú, kristni, þjóðtrú*. Reykjavík: Bókaútgáfan Þjóðsaga.

Jón Ma. Ásgeirsson. (2009). Gjörningar og galdur í frumkristni: Af postulum og seiðurum. Printed in *Studia Theologica Islandica 29*. Reykjavík: Guðfræðistofnun - Skálholtsútgáfan.

Jón Ólafsson (1992). *Reisubók*. Reykjavík: Mál og menning.

Ketils saga hœngs (1954). Fornaldar sögur Norðurlanda II. Reykjavík: Íslendingasagnaútgáfan.

Keyworth, D. (2007). *Troublesome Corpses: Vampires & Revenants From Antiquity to the Present*. Southend on Sea: Desert Island Books.

Kjalnesinga saga (1986). Íslendinga sögur XII. Reykjavík: Íslendingasagnaútgáfan.

Kjartan G. Ottósson. (1983). *Fróðárundur í Eyrbyggju*. Studia Islandica 42. Reykjavík: Bókmenntafræðistofnun Háskóla Íslands - Bókaútgáfa Menningarsjóðs.

Konungs skuggsjá (1955). Reykjavík: H.F. Leiftur.

Kormáks saga (1939). Íslenzk fornrit VIII. Reykjavík: Hið íslenzka fornritafélag.

Kormak's saga (1997). Translated by Rory McTurk. Printed in *The Complete Sagas of Icelanders I*. Reykjavík: Leifur Eiríksson Publishing.

Kumlbúa þáttr (1986). Íslendinga sögur IV. Reykjavík: Íslendingasagnaútgáfan.

Larrington, Carolyne. (1995.). Leizla rannveigar: Gender and polidics in the otherworld vision. Printed in *Medium Aevum*, Volume 64. Oxford.

Laxdœla saga (1934). Íslenzk fornrit V. Reykjavík: Hið íslenzka fornritafélag.

Le Goff, Jacques. (2005). Hinar löngu miðaldir. Printed in *Ritið 3: Miðaldir*. Reykjavík: Hugvísindastofnun Háskóla Íslands.

Leslie, Helen F. (2009). Border crossings: Landscape and the other world in the fornaldarsögur. Printed in *Scripta Islandica 60*.

Stockholm: Almquist och Wiksell.

Lönnroth, Lars. (1990). *Two Norse-Icelandic Studies: Sponsors, Writers and Readers of Early Norse Literature and A Road Paved with Legends*. Litteraturvetenskapliga Institutionen – Göteborgs Universitet.

Lüthi, M. (1992). *Das europäische Volksmärchen: Form und Wesen*. Tübingen.

Magnús Rafnsson (2006). Hvaða galdur? ólík viðhorf alþýðu og yfirvalda. Printed in Torfi H. Tulinius (Ed.), *Galdramenn. Galdrar og samfélag á miðöldum: Greinar frá ráðstefnu Vestfjarða á miðöldum, Laugarbóli 1. og 2. september 2006*. Reykjavík: Hugvísindastofnun Háskóla Íslands.

Már Jónsson. (2008). Ákvæði jónsbókar um galdra. uppruni og áhrif. Printed in *Galdramenn. Galdrar og samfélag á miðöldum: Greinar frá ráðstefnu Vestfjarða á miðöldum, Laugarbóli 1. og 2. september 2006*. Reykjavík: Hugvísindastofnun Háskóla Íslands.

Matthías Viðar Sæmundsson (1996). *Galdur á brennuöld*. Reykjavík: Storð.

Mitchell, Stephen A. (1998). Anaphrodisiac charms in the nordic middle ages: Impotence, infertility, and magic. Printed in *The Norwegian Journal of Folklore 38*. Norveg.

Mitchell, Stephen A. (2006). Pactum cum diabolo og galdur á norðurlöndum. Printed in Torfi H. Tulinius (Ed.), *Galdramenn. Galdrar og samfélag á miðöldum: Greinar frá ráðstefnu Vestfjarða á miðöldum, Laugarbóli 1. og 2. september 2006*. Reykjavík: Hugvísindastofnun Háskóla Íslands.

Mitchell, Stephen A. (2009). The supernatural and the fornaldarsögur: The case of ketils saga hœngs. Printed in Agneta Ney,

159

Ármann Jakobsson, Annette Lassen (Ed.), *Fornaldarsagaerne: Myter og virkelighed*. København: Museum Tusculanums Forlag - Københavns Universitet.

Mitchell, Stephen A. (2011). *Witchcraft and Magic in the Nordic Middle Ages*. Philadelphia - Oxford: University of Pennsylvania Press.

Mohrmann, Ch. (1955). *Latin vulgaire, latin des Chrétiens, latin médiéval*. Paris.

Mundal, Else (2006). The treatment of the supernatural and the fantastic in different saga genres. Printed in *The fantastic in Old Norse/Icelandic literature. Sagas and the British isles: preprint papers of the 13th International Saga Conference Durham and York, 6th-12th August, 2006*. Durham: The Centre for Medieval and Renaissance Studies, Durham University.

Nordvig, Mathias. (2011). Lord and monster: Snorri's explanation of heathenry in ynglinga saga in connection with óðinn, njǫrðr and freyr as the 'founding fathers' of the ynglings. Unpublished article, part of the curriculum for the course Old Norse mythology in medieval and modern times.

Ólína Þorvarðardóttir (2000). *Brennuöldin*. Reykjavík: Háskólaútgáfan.

Orm Storolfsson's tale (1997). Translated by Matthew Driscoll. Printed in *The Complete Sagas of Icelanders III*. Reykjavík: Leifur Eiríksson Publishing.

Orms þáttr Stórólfssonar (1986). Íslendinga sögur XI. Reykjavík: Íslendingasagnaútgáfan.

Physiologus (1938). Ithaca, New York: Cornell University Press.

Píslarsaga sr. Jóns Magnússonar (2001). Reykjavík: Mál og menning.

Power, Rosemary. (1985). Journeys to the otherworld in the icelandic fornaldarsögur. Printed in *Folklore vol. 96*. London: Folklore Society.

Ragnars saga loðbrókar (1985). Printed in *Völsunga saga og Ragnars saga loðbrókar*. Reykjavík: Mál og menning.

Reed Kline, Naomi. (2005). The world of strange races. Printed in *Monsters, Marvels and Miracles: Imaginary Journeys and Landscapes in the Middle Ages*. Odense: University Press of Southern Denmark.

Sävborg, Daniel. (2009). Avstånd, gräns och förundran. Printed in *Greppaminni. Rit til heiðurs Vésteini Ólasyni sjötugum*. Reykjavík: Hið íslenska bókmenntafélag.

Sävborg, Daniel. (2012). Scandinavian folk legends and post-classical íslendingasögur. Forthcoming.

Schier, Kurt (1981). Zur mythologie der snorra edda: Einige quellenprobleme. Printed in *Speculum norroneum. Norse studies in memory of Gabriel Turville-Petre*. Odense: Odense University Press.

Schjødt, Jens Peter (2007). Hvad er det i grunden, vi rekonstruerer? Printed in *Religionsvidenskapeligt Tidsskrift nr. 50*.

Schjødt, Jens Peter. (2009). Kan myten være virkelighed? Printed in Agneta Ney, Ármann Jakobsson, Annette Lassen (Ed.), *Fornaldarsagaerne: Myter og virkelighed*. København: Museum Tusculanums Forlag - Københavns Universitet.

Sigurður Nordal. (1993). *Fornar menntir I*. Reykjavík: Almenna bókafélagið.

Sigurður Nordal, Guðni Jónsson. (Ed.) (1938). *Íslenzk fornrit III: Borgfirðingasögur*. Íslenzka fornritaútgáfan.

Simek, Rudolf. (1992). *Erde und Kosmos im Mittelalter. Das Weltbild vor Kolumbus*, pp. 55–73. München.

Simek, Rudolf. (1993). *Hugtök og heiti í norrænni goðafræði*. Reykjavík: Heimskringla - háskólaforlag Máls og menningar.

Simek, Rudolf. (2009). The medieval icelandic world view and the theory of the two cultures. Printed in *Gripla XX*. Stofnun Árna Magnússonar á Íslandi.

Snorra-Edda (2002). Mál og menning.

Svarfdæla saga (1986). Íslendinga sögur VIII. Reykjavík: Íslendingasagnaútgáfan.

Sverrir Jakobsson. (2005). *Við og veröldin*. Reykjavík: Háskólaútgáfan.

Sverrir Jakobsson. (2006). On the road to paradise: "austrvegr" in the icelandic imagination. Printed in *The fantastic in Old Norse/Icelandic literature. Sagas and the British isles: preprint papers of the 13th International Saga Conference Durham and York, 6th-12th August, 2006*. The Centre for Medieval and Renaissance Studies, Durham University.

Sverrir Jakobsson. (2008). Galdur og forspá í ríkisvaldslausu samfélagi. Printed in *Galdramenn. Galdrar og samfélag á miðöldum: Greinar frá ráðstefnu Vestfjarða á miðöldum, Laugarbóli 1. og 2. september 2006*. Reykjavík: Hugvísindastofnun Háskóla Íslands.

Sverrir Jakobsson. (2010). Myndirnar af heiminum. um heimsbelli, heimskringlur og vínlandsferðir norrænna manna. Printed in Einar H. Guðmundsson, Eyja Margrét Brynjarsdóttir, Gunnar Karlsson, Orri Vésteinsson, Sverrir Jakobsson (Ed.), *Vísindave-fur. Ritgerðasafn til heiðurs Þorsteini Vilhjálmssyni sjötugum*. Reykjavík: Hið íslenska bókmenntafélag.

Sverrir Tómasson. (1988). *Formálar íslenskra sagnaritara á miðöldum*. Reykjavík: Stofnun Árna Magnússonar á Íslandi.

Sverrir Tómasson. (2001). Ferðir þessa heims og annars. paradís - ódáinsakur - vínland í íslenskum ferðalýsingum miðalda. Printed in *Gripla XII*. Reykjavík: Stofnun Árna Magnússonar á Íslandi.

Swift, J. (2011). *Reisubók Gúllívers*. Reykjavík: Mál og menning.

The Middle English Physiologus (1991). Published for the Early English Text Society by the Oxford University Press.

The saga of Bjorn, champion of the Hitardal people (1997). Translated by Alison Finlay. Printed in *The Complete Sagas of Icelanders I*. Reykjavík: Leifur Eiríksson Publishing.

The saga of Finnbogi the mighty (1997). Translated by John Kennedy. Printed in *The Complete Sagas of Icelanders III*. Reykjavík: Leifur Eiríksson Publishing.

The saga of Grettir the strong (1997). Translated by Bernard Scudder. Printed in *The Complete Sagas of Icelanders II*. Reykjavík: Leifur Eiríksson Publishing.

The saga of the Greenlanders (1997). Translated by Keneva Kunz. Printed in *The Complete Sagas of Icelanders I*. Reykjavík: Leifur Eiríksson Publishing.

The saga of the people of Eyri (1997). Translated by Judy Quinn. Printed in *The Complete Sagas of Icelanders V*. Reykjavík: Leifur Eiríksson Publishing.

The saga of the people of Fljotsdal (1997). Translated by John Porter. Printed in *The Complete Sagas of Icelanders IV*. Reykjavík: Leifur Eiríksson Publishing.

The saga of the people of Kjalarnes (1997). Translated by Robert Cook. Printed in *The Complete Sagas of Icelanders III*. Reykjavík: Leifur Eiríksson Publishing.

The saga of the people of Laxardal (1997). Translated by Keneva Kunz. Printed in *The Complete Sagas of Icelanders V*. Reykjavík: Leifur Eiríksson Publishing.

The saga of the people of Vatnsdal (1997). Translated by Andrew Wawn. Printed in *The Complete Sagas of Icelanders IV*. Reykjavík: Leifur Eiríksson Publishing.

The tale of the mountain-dweller (1997). Translated by Marvin Taylor. Printed in *The Complete Sagas of Icelanders II*. Reykjavík: Leifur Eiríksson Publishing.

Todorov, Tzvetan. (1975). *The Fantastic. A Structural Approach to a Literary Genre*. Ithaca: Cornell University Press.

Torfi H. Tulinius. (1990). Landafræði og flokkun fornsagna. Printed in *Skáldskaparmál 1*. Reykjavík: Stafaholt hf.

Torfi H. Tulinius. (1999). Framliðnir feður: Um forneskju og frásagnarlist í eyrbyggju, eglu og grettlu. Printed in Haraldur Bessason og Baldur Hafstað (Ed.), *Heiðin minni. Greinar um fornar bókmenntir*. Reykjavík: Heimskringla - háskólaforlag Máls og menningar.

Torfi H. Tulinius. (2008). Galdar og samfélag í aldanna rás. Printed in *Galdramenn. Galdrar og samfélag á miðöldum: Greinar frá ráðstefnu Vestfjarða á miðöldum, Laugarbóli 1. og 2. september 2006.* Reykjavík: Hugvísindastofnun Háskóla Íslands.

Torfi H. Tulinius. (2009). The self as other: Iceland and the culture of southern europe in the middle ages. Printed in *Gripla XX.* Stofnun Árna Magnússonar á Íslandi.

Unnur Jökulsdóttir. (2007). *Hefurðu séð huldufólk?* Reykjavík: Mál og menning.

Vatnsdœla saga (1939). Íslenzk fornrit VIII. Reykjavík: Hið íslenzka fornritafélag.

Vésteinn Ólason. (1999). Rímur og miðaldarómantík: Um úrvinnslu goðsagnaminna og goðsagnamynstra í íslenskum rómönsum á síðmiðöldum. Printed in *Heiðin minni. Greinar um fornar bókmenntir.* Reykjavík: Heimskringla - háskólaforlag Máls og menningar.

Vésteinn Ólason. (2003). The un/grateful dead - from baldr to bægifótr. Printed in *Old Norse Myths, Literature and Society.* Viborg: University Press of Southern Denmark.

Vésteinn Ólason. (2007). The fantastic element in fourteenth century íslendingasögur. a survey. Printed in *Gripla XVIII.* Reykjavík: Stofnun Árna Magnússonar á Íslandi.

Wellendorf, Jonas. (2009). *Kristelig visionslitteratur i norrøn tradition.* Oslo: Novus forlag.

Williamsen, E. A. (2005). Boundaries of difference in the vínland sagas. Printed in *Scandinavian Studies 77.*

Þiðreks saga af Bern (1962). Reykjavík: Íslendingasagnaútgáfan.

Þorskfirðinga saga (1986). Íslendinga sögur IV. Reykjavík: Íslendingasagnaútgáfan.

Þorsteinn Vilhjálmsson. (1986). *Heimsmynd á hverfanda hveli*. Reykjavík: Mál og menning.

Þorsteinn Vilhjálmsson. (2001). Navigation and vínland. Printed in
A. Wawn and Þórunn Sigurðardóttir (Eds.), *Approaches to Vín-
land. A conference on the written and archaeological sources for the
Norse settlements in the North-Atlantic region and exploration of
America. The Nordic House, Reykjavík. 9-11 August 1999*. Reyk-
javík: Sigurður Nordal Institute.